101+ Tips and Tricks Every Prop Maker Should Know

In *101+ Tips and Tricks Every Prop Maker Should Know*, Utah Shakespeare Festival's Properties Director Ben Hohman explains tricks of the trade generally not taught in schools, but essential for prop makers working on the job.

With tips and tricks divided into subject categories like carpentry, prop math, soft goods, upholstery, finishing, crafts and effects, and tools, the book breaks this knowledge down so that makers and prop managers can easily access the information, learn the skills, and be better prepared and more useful to any shop they work in. Each tip or trick is clearly introduced, features a relevant example of how it is useful, and includes step-by-step instructions. The book also features interviews and tips from prop makers across the creative industries, showcasing different techniques and need-to-know skills, and a glossary of prop terms that will help readers navigate the day-to-day of the prop shop.

This book is written for theatrical prop artisans, prop managers, technical theatre students, and anyone who has an interest in prop building or backstage theatrical knowledge. Whether they are novice prop builders or seasoned professionals with decades of experience, this book will provide readers with a wealth of practical information that will serve them in their craft for many years to come.

Ben Hohman is the Properties Director at the Utah Shakespeare Festival. He is active in USITT, Vice President of The Society of Props Managers (S*P*M), and adjunct faculty at Southern Utah University. He has worked in regional theatre for the past 31 years both at Actors Theatre in Louisville, Kentucky (4 years) and at the Utah Shakespeare Festival (31 years and counting). He also has worked freelance, and as a co-owner of an event company that designed, produced, and built pageants, scenery, and props for ballet and theatrical productions, as well as floats for parades.

BEN HOHMAN

101+ Tips and Tricks Every Prop Maker Should Know

NEW YORK AND LONDON

Designed cover image: Main prop shop area at the Utah Shakespeare Festival, photo by Ben Hohman.

First published 2025
by Routledge
605 Third Avenue, New York, NY 10158

and by Routledge
4 Park Square, Milton Park, Abingdon, Oxon, OX14 4RN

Routledge is an imprint of the Taylor & Francis Group, an informa business

© 2025 Ben Hohman

The right of Ben Hohman to be identified as author of this work has been asserted in accordance with sections 77 and 78 of the Copyright, Designs and Patents Act 1988.

All rights reserved. No part of this book may be reprinted or reproduced or utilised in any form or by any electronic, mechanical, or other means, now known or hereafter invented, including photocopying and recording, or in any information storage or retrieval system, without permission in writing from the publishers.

Trademark notice: Product or corporate names may be trademarks or registered trademarks, and are used only for identification and explanation without intent to infringe.

ISBN: 978-1-032-47010-8 (hbk)
ISBN: 978-1-032-47008-5 (pbk)
ISBN: 978-1-003-38418-2 (ebk)

DOI: 10.4324/9781003384182

Typeset in Joanna MT
by codeMantra

This book is Dedicated to Marielle Boneau
and to Walter Stark

Contents

Foreword ix
Preface xv
Acknowledgments xviii

Carpentry/Basic shop work **One** 1
Prop math **Two** 14
Soft goods/Sewing **Three** 24
Upholstery/Drapery **Four** 34
Painting and finishing **Five** 50
Crafts and effects **Six** 63
Specialized tools of the trade **Seven** 83
Prop reference **Eight** 107
Prop knowledge **Nine** 128
Prop perspectives **Ten** 141
Tips from the wider world of props **Eleven** 155
Words of the trade (Glossary) **Twelve** 165

Index 173

Foreword by Walter Stark, Senior Artisan from 2012 to 2022

In the early years, 2012–2015, of my stints at the Utah Shakespeare Festival (USF) Prop Shop, a company-wide meeting was held in May, marking the start of the current production season. Mostly, the meeting was a welcome to the artistic staff and an opportunity for past members to get re-acquainted. The primary founder of the USF, Mr. Fred Adams, commonly gave a combination of history and pep talk as part of his welcome speech, which was always fun and warming to me. At some point in his usually very animated talk, Adams would begin asking various of the support staff to stand up. I can't recall the order he used, but each support group, Props, Costumers, Set Carpenters, Fight Instructors, etc., was asked to stand and remain standing. I think the actors were usually asked to stand either first or last. Based on all those artistic groups standing by the end of his requests, Fred would estimate the fraction of the total representing the non-actor portion of the group; he used 80% often. Adams would then tell the Actors present to remember that 80% of the applause at the end of any performance should be bestowed upon the non-actor portion of the artistic staff. I personally very much appreciated that view, and I believe that point was well taken by the entire artistic staff. Sadly, Fred Adams died in 2020, and this particular pep talk, among many other contributions, will be sorely missed by the USF performing company.

One can look up the Festival Organization, for example, in the back of the Souvenir Program, for a high-level list of the creators of a theater production:

Playwrights	Scenery and Scenic Artists
Directors	Properties
Designers	Displays
Actors	Costumes
Choreographers	Make-up
Stage Management	Music
Special Services	Lighting and Electrics

Those in the right column make up the efforts that create the overt and subtle ambiance felt, heard, and seen in a performance, making the theatrical production an immersive experience and providing the uniqueness of any single production of a particular playwright.

I have begun to think of the support functions in the right column as volumes in a sorcerer's library of magic; think Prospero of *The Tempest*. Each volume holds the secrets, tricks, and spells which, when applied to audience members, draw them more into the story, perhaps in a manner not always fully recognized by the patron. Not all tricks and spells are used in every play, and it is up to the sorcery practitioner to apply what they feel will be helpful in creating a needed ambiance.

Examining how much the craft support makes the play is a thought I have had before. It is not at all my place to say which of the supporting crafts is the most critical; each contributes to some degree. I came to the Props Shop almost by accident: In the 2011 Camp Shakespeare sessions, Properties Director Ben Hohman gave the Shakespeare Campers his usual entertaining overview lecture of stage properties for the 2011 season. As I listened to Ben describe his group's solution to individually attaching something like 40,000 leaves to branches of a tree on the set of *A Midsummer Night's Dream*, I was struck by the similarity of the solution approach to this problem to work in my own scientific profession. I had been retired for almost 11 years then and mused that it could be fun to try volunteering at such tasks. I had some knowledge and experience in furniture making, woodworking, and other crafts, so I pursued an application to work in the Properties Department. Ben took a gamble on me.

For the 2012 USF theater season, I found myself engaged in Properties, or Props, for short, and working for a Props Director, Ben Hohman, who really knows his stuff. It might be natural for me to think Props are the most important supporting theater craft, but the reality is that all the supporting crafts have knowledgeable leaders and deserve similar accolades. So, of the supporting crafts, those beyond the playwright, the dialogs, and the actors, the Hohman how-to book, and I, in this foreword, will focus on theater Props, where I have worked a small fraction of the past 11 years, and where for around 30 years, Ben Hohman has worked, eaten, slept and breathed Props, gathering up the tips and tricks he presents in this book.

At the beginning of each theater season at the annual Utah Shakespeare Festival (USF), Hohman gathers up those he has chosen to work in the Props Main Shop out on Cedar City's Bulldog Drive and reminds them of the nature of Theater Props using his moving van analogy: if the theater fixed set and scenery represent the equivalent of a new house for you, then stage props are all the items you might put into a moving van to take to your new home. What you bring in the van converts the bare new house into your new home, replete with your styles and memories. Props do the same for the stage set, making the set feel and look like what the playwright and the director believe it should be.

The individual props necessary to do this can span a broad range of needs, and some props may exist only in the minds of the playwright and director. As I understand it, the Props Director, his Props Supervisor(s), and the performance Director meet to discuss the performance Director's vision of the performance; the Scenic Designer may attend as well. Out of these discussions eventually comes a shopping list of all the stage properties required to help create the desired ambiance of the play.

A goodly part of the shopping list can be withdrawn mainly from the existing stock of USF props. Some stock props can be used as is; others may require some minor re-purposing effort, like different paint or perhaps re-upholstering. Sometimes, the re-purposing is major and even might exist only in the mind of the Props Director, whose clever re-imagining of an old battery-powered golf cart came to life as an operational but somewhat smaller than real-life, stage-going Model T Ford car that was quite the hit in the 2021 USF version of *Ragtime*.

Then, there are some props on the shopping list that don't exist at the USF Props warehouse and, further, are not available from Hohman's Props colleagues at theaters all across the whole country. Construction of these needed props, if not too expensive for a play's props budget, will take place at the Props Shop by the Props Artisans hired for the theater season.

From a simple bench to elaborate dinner tables, from a smoke-tooting, light-flashing furniture calliope meant to disguise an electronic keyboard as well as entertain the *Scapin* audience, to a simple hand-carved sign guiding the way in a stage forest of *To Kill a Mockingbird*, from a gold-leafed royal blue sword rack to a fancy throne that ages across a chronological series of Shakespeare's history plays; a golden cash register with a key activated by the actor to ring its bell in time to the music in *The Cocoanuts*; even a radio-controlled tumbleweed that bounced along the street of a San Francisco-like town in one version of *A Comedy of Errors*.

All of these creations were developed and fabricated by Props Artisans in the Bulldog Road Props workshop. While the larger furniture or moveable scenery items often had construction blueprints for guidance, many also sprung mostly from the minds and hands of the Artisans and the Props Director and Supervisors. And even blueprints weren't a saving grace: more than one Props Artisan had the experience of their creation returning from its initial delivery to the stage for rehearsals, with a note that it was too wide, or too high, or maybe the wrong color; sometimes there was considerable re-work necessary to make the item fit the stage and the play.

Many of the Artisans working at the USF have academic training as well as on-the-job experience; all seem eager to practice their trade and to gain more experience. And whether or not they know at the outset of a new USF theater season, they will learn here at the hands of a bona fide master of theater properties, Ben Hohman.

When I was first engaged to work for Props Construction at the 2012 USF theater season, I had a mixed bag of fabrication talents, all of which were modest capabilities. I have had a long infatuation with internal combustion things like lawnmowers, race cars, and motorcycles. I considered myself a knowledgeable mechanic for such motorized vehicles and had a fine set of associated tools with which I could further hone my skills. I also had often indulged in the fabrication of wooden items, from bookshelves to instrument cases or cabinetry for tools; I was no stranger to a radial arm saw. And finally, my professional life as a research materials scientist exposed me to the very precise measurement, construction, and fabrication techniques that are often associated with scientific research efforts. While I certainly wasn't a neophyte with tools when I first appeared at the Bulldog Props Shop, I had no idea how many more tips and tricks I was going pick up over the next decade or so. (Or even that I was going to enjoy making Props so much or to continue making them over that same time interval.)

While all of us Props Artisans had different fabrication experiences, we all were to grow through capabilities learned in the USF Props Shop. Hohman and his Supervisors always handed out individual assignments in a way that could capitalize on our existing competencies yet also would be challenging enough to make us think a bit. It also was usually at this point that, if needed, we would be introduced to and instructed on the shortcuts or tricks useful or needed to complete an assignment. I can truly state only for myself, but it is likely that all Artisans in every USF theater season learned at least a few of the Hohman Prop Tips and Tricks found in this book.

Of the many satisfying memories I have of my times working at the USF, the more gratifying and recurrent dealt with projects I was given wherein I initially was stumped as to how to proceed, or, after working and thinking some hours, I realized that my approach was not working. Often, it would take repeated approaches or a few more hours or days until I came up with a satisfying solution that fit into the needed schedule. Sometimes, the rehearsal schedule forced the chosen solution! In any case, I was intellectually gratified and pleased that I had created such a solution. I'm certain that the other USF Artisans I have worked with have been similarly pleased with most of their creations. These creations resulted from some wondrous combination of the Props Director's shopping list and guidance, the creative juices flowing in an excited Props Artisan, and the fabrication techniques known by or learned at the USF Props facilities. Many of the tips and techniques in the book you are holding contributed to this creativity.

I have to say that many times, my props creations were probably over-built to something like military construction specs, which was mostly totally unnecessary (except when actors were dancing or jumping on some piece of furniture I had constructed). Hohman and his experienced Supervisors often hurried along the completion of my creations by firmly telling me, "That's good enough!" They had the experience I lacked in knowing how Props would be viewed and received by patrons in the audience.

Some of the formal Props training my Artisan colleagues had received addressed an area in which I had essentially no experience other than making an item look new, well-made, and attractive. My trained Artisan colleagues, especially Hohman, were often far more capable at "making the appearance," by which I mean making something look old, aged, distressed, well-used, rich, poor, common, or any state other than brand new or freshly painted. I often consulted with Hohman or my Artisan colleagues for advice on "making the appearance." Still, later in my ten seasons, I often just turned over my mechanical creations to another Artisan to complete the "making the appearance" details.

Whether by job assignment or his own feelings on the issue, it has been obvious that Hohman takes seriously his educational duties relative to his Props Artisan charges each season. I saw his concern for expanding their knowledge and safety every day at work in the Props Shop; almost every working day morning, he told charming stories, episodes in some cases from his working past, that illustrated some safety-related issue a Props Artisan might encounter, and the proper steps to be taken to ameliorate or eliminate the issue.

Sadly, Walter passed away in January of 2023 after a second bout with stomach cancer, just a week after writing this for me.

Image 0.1 A photo of Walter Stark working in the Utah Shakespeare Festival Prop Shop.
Source: Photo by the author.

Preface

I have had the idea of writing a book about props for a long time, and I could never quite hit upon the right topic or way of presenting my thoughts until I was approached about pitching a specific idea for a prop book to this publisher. I mulled a few ideas around and then pitched them to Walter to see what he thought (I have always respected and admired Walter for taking such a leap into a new field so late in his life). He thought all the ideas were interesting but considered the idea of presenting little tips and tricks was right on because, as he mentioned in his forward, that was the part of the process that always fascinated and inspired him. It was during that discussion that I asked him if I got the contract to write a book and if he would be willing to write the forward. He was initially hesitant and felt I knew other prop people with more experience who could do a better job. I told him to think about it, and we could discuss it again later. About two weeks later, he came to me and said he had considered it and would be honored to write the forward. I got the contract and began the writing process; little did I know Walter started as well, and before I had even turned in my first chapter for approval, the forward was written. I did not know at the time that Walter's stomach cancer had returned in a much more severe way. He sent me the completed forward and then, a week later, called to ask if it was okay and if I had any corrections or things I wanted him to change. I told him I thought it was great as it was, and if anything came up, we could make some edits later. That was when he dropped the bomb that wouldn't be possible as the doctors had given him only a few weeks to live. I was devastated and told Walter not to worry about the forward, that he should be with his family and the forward would be fine as it was, just to put it out of his head and spend what little time he had left being Walter with those he loved. Writing this book has been more challenging than I thought it would be. I almost threw in the towel numerous times, feeling I didn't have all the knowledge I pretend to when I am at work, but every time that thought came into my head, I thought of the last time Walter was in Cedar City and met up with Marielle and me for dinner. As we talked, he said the most remarkable thing.

> I wish I had a chance earlier in my career to have worked for you because the creativity, ingenuity, and the attitude of 'let's give it a try and see what happens' that you share with your staff would have made me a better scientist.

That pushed me through. It may not all be "right," or all "make sense" but it works, and that is what really counts. I miss Walter and hope he is proud of this work, and I am so glad he contributed to it.

I want to add a few words about the one thing I have realized is probably the most important in our job as a prop maker. We are storytellers, just like the playwright who wrote the script and the director who has a vision for how they want to tell that story, so too do we bring foresight and our artistic ability to the art of storytelling. We are working with the other disciplines to create an environment where that story in this iteration can take place for our audience. Sometimes the perfect prop, or most historically accurate one, doesn't work in the telling, so we work with the designer, director, actor, etc., to find the object that does work, that conveys the meaning needed to help clarify and focus the story as much as we are able. As much fun and heartache that we have in trying to get all the dressing right, the furniture not to squeak and bear the weight of the actors, making sure the book they pick up is just the right size, color, and weight, often that minutia is not important in the long run, always take a moment to step back and look at the bigger picture. Does it contribute to the story positively and directly? If so, then you are on the right path.

Many times, during the process of putting this book together I have asked myself: Am I qualified to write this book? As much as any prop master, prop supervisor, or prop maker out there is, I suppose. I have spent 30 years at the Utah Shakespeare Festival working on over 288 productions. Along the way, I have been taught many things by the artisans, designers, and other technicians I work with. I have found new ways of doing things by researching or stumbled upon a new solution for a problem. This book is a collection of many of those things. I tried to break them into reasonable sections so that similar items are grouped together. I generally give a real-world example of the problem along with the steps to create the solution and some general tips along the way. This is, of course, not a comprehensive guide, but just things that I have figured out along my journey. There will always be more, and I look forward to hearing from you, the readers, about tips and tricks you have learned as we continue down this crazy, wacky, fun prop road together.

Acknowledgments

This book has been a labor of love, well, at least a labor. I could not have done it without the support of my excellent partner in crime, Marielle Boneau. We met at the Utah Shakespeare Festival 27 years ago and we have developed into an incredible team both at work and in life. She lifts me up and supports all my crazy ideas, and I could not ask for a better fellow adventurer.

A special thanks to the Utah Shakespeare Festival, for providing me with so many opportunities year-in and year-out to learn, grow, and experiment, while producing some pretty amazing theater for the last 30+ years. Also for letting me use many examples from my work at the Festival throughout this book, and for the use of two amazing production photos in Chapter Seven.

I would also like to thank the hundreds of artisans and prop supervisors I have worked with at the Utah Shakespeare Festival and elsewhere during my career. I hope I have taught you as much as you have taught me.

Thanks to all the prop people I have met through the Society of Prop Managers (S*P*M) for always supporting and sharing within the group and making all of us better at this crazy job. A special shout out to the prop people who contributed their ideas to Chapter Eleven of this book. I wish I had room for dozens more, but maybe someday, when I have a website, it can be a monthly feature....

To Kelly Mangan, my technical editor, friend, and mentor, from early in my career, for reading this thing in draft form and giving me many great suggestions to improve it.

To the editorial staff at Focal Press, thank you for reaching out and taking a chance on this long-time prop person/first-time writer.

To my family for letting me get into the theater and never judging me too harshly (at least not to my face).

As I said in the introduction, I hope this book is not the end but the beginning. I plan to continue to learn new things and to share those lessons with the prop world. Prop on my friends, prop on.

Carpentry/Basic shop work

One

Carpentry is an important aspect of prop work. While some shops do not have a carpentry shop or very many woodworking tools, knowing some basic carpentry skills will help solve many prop problems. There is often a misconception in the "outside world" that furniture is just purchased and put onstage, while on the rare occasion that is true, more often, we modify, strengthen, or adjust the furniture to fit the needs of the production. If given the opportunity to take a woodworking class at some point in your career, I highly recommend it. What follows are some tips and tricks that will help in specific carpentry situations.

1 FINDING THE CENTER OF A CIRCULAR OBJECT QUICKLY

We often need to find the center of a circular or oval object. There are mathematical ways to do this, but they can be time-consuming and confusing. There are also commercially available center-finding jigs (we have one in the shop), but often find it is not nearly big enough for the circles we are working with. Because of that we built a large center finding jig to make it easier and faster to quickly find the center of the object in question. (See Image 1.1.) It is comprised of a rectangular piece of plywood with a 45-degree notch cut out of the middle of one of the long sides, attached to that plywood at a 90-degree perpendicular angle is a two-foot long piece of one-by running through the middle of the notch, creating a 90-degree angle aligned with the middle of the notch. When we slide the notch against a circular object and draw a line along the edge of the one-by. Move the jig to another spot on the circle/oval and repeat the process. Where the lines cross will be the center of that object.

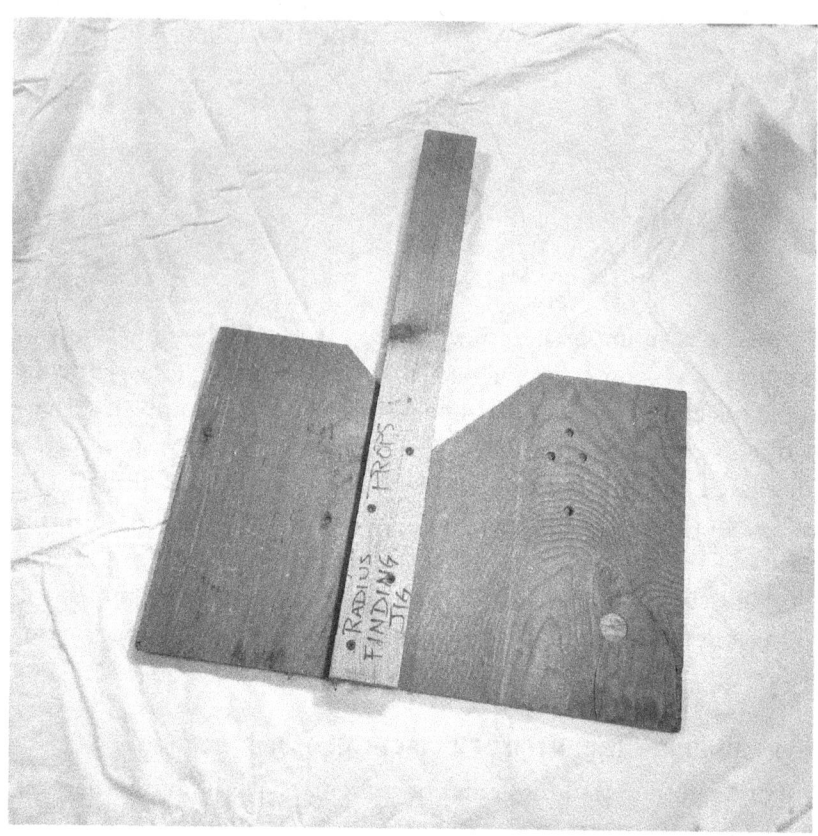

Image 1.1 A photo of our shop-built center finding jig.
Source: Photo by the author.

2 THE FRENCH CLEAT

In many productions swapping out set dressing during quick scene changes is essential. One way to make this easier and ensure the set dressing is level and secure is with the use of the french cleat. The usefulness of this simple hanging/mounting method cannot be overstated, particularly in a rotating rep situation where we are doing full changeovers of scenery and props multiple times a day for weeks and weeks. A french cleat uses a piece of wood that you cut lengthwise into two parts at a 45-degree angle. You then mount one piece of the wood horizontally to the work of art or the object you want to hang. You attach the corresponding piece to the wall or surface on which you want to hang the thing – aligning them so that the object nestles into the angled piece on that surface, so the two 45-degree angles interlock. You can make the cleat any length you want to help with the support and levelness of the hung object. One great thing about a french cleat rather than a typical hanging method for art is that the french cleat will keep the art or object straighter over time because the object does not hang from a single point. Another great feature is that it is secured well; the french cleat can support a lot of weight, providing stability to an object. There is a great deal of debate about how the french cleat got its name, but the explanation I heard that makes the most sense is that it doesn't have anything to do with France but more with the English verb "french," which is to cut into thin strips (Image 1.2).

On a production of Clue, we had a spinning/pivoting wall; on one side was a portrait gallery where one portrait swung out to reveal a wall safe. The other side of the wall was the billiard room. During one scene in the portrait gallery, the wall safe needed to be opened, and a large bag needed to be stuffed into the safe; however, the wall was only two inches thick. To accomplish this, we mounted a dart board on a

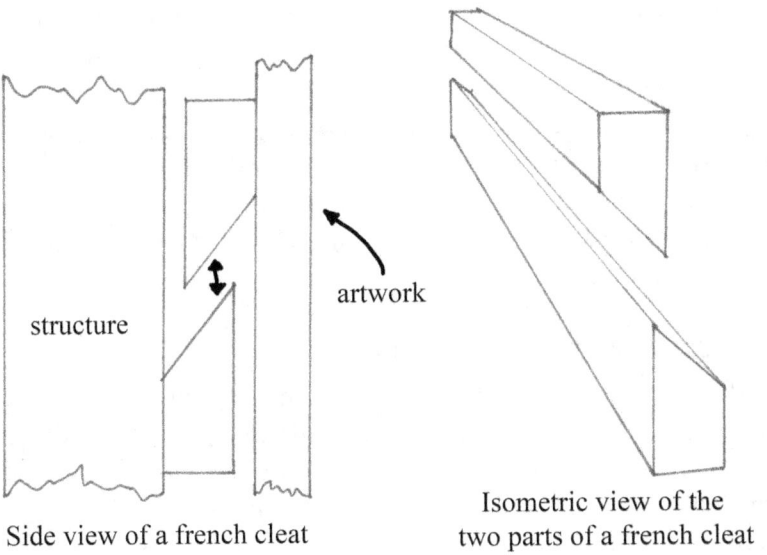

Side view of a french cleat   Isometric view of the two parts of a french cleat

Image 1.2 Illustrations of a french cleat.
Source: Illustrations by the author.

french cleat on the billiard room side of the wall. During the scene in question, the crew removed the dartboard and held up a black laundry basket; when the safe was opened and the bag stuffed inside, it fell through the wall and into the basket. Once that was accomplished, the dartboard was rehung over the opening, and the wall was spun to reveal the billiard room with no visible method for stuffing the bag into the safe.

In another example, on the same show, we had to mount a kitchen cabinet on the wall in the kitchen, but the kitchen wall unit needed to fly for storage of the show due to the rep. The kitchen cabinet stuck out too far and would not clear other units in the fly loft. So, we hung the cabinet with a french cleat. The cabinet was on the wall during the performance, but during the changeover, the crew lifted it off the cleat and stored it on the deck with other furniture items from the show, and the wall was then clear to fly out.

3 STOPPING WOOD BLOWOUT

A common problem in woodworking is drilling a hole in a piece of wood and having the side opposite where you started drilling blow out as the bit comes through. This leaves a rough edge to the hole and a splintering out of the wood, which can be unsightly and difficult to patch or clean up. A simple way around this dilemma is using a sacrificial block of wood. If you place the piece of wood you are drilling on top of the sacrificial piece (Clamping the pieces together leads to greater success) and then drill the hole, 95% of the time, the hole will be drilled cleanly because the drill bit continues into the sacrificial piece and the force of the two pieces together keeps the piece you are drilling from blowing out.

4 QUICK WAYS TO FIX LOOSE JOINTS

We often find that our antique furniture gets very dry in our environment (as we are in a desert). This leads to the joints becoming loose and the furniture feeling rickety and unstable. Sometimes, just throwing some glue into the joints and clamping it will solve the problem, but more often than not, more is needed. We have found two methods that can help strengthen an old joint and make it much more secure. So, when an actor stands on the 100-year-old chair, no one is worried about them ending up in a heap on the floor with pieces of the chair scattered around them. Method one is to drill a hole into the joint and install a dowel pin with lots of wood glue to help keep the pieces together. The second method is to predrill a pilot hole into the joint in question and put a substantial wood screw into the joint. We recess the hole slightly so we can cap it with a piece of dowel, sand it smooth and stain it out so we don't see the screw.

5 THE AMAZING POCKET SCREW

To speed up the construction of furniture and hide the hardware, we also often incorporate the use of the Kreg jig, or in more layperson's terms, we use pocket screws. A pocket screw is a hidden screw on the inside of a butt joint that is screwed in at a steep angle allowing it to pull the two pieces of material together and, with the addition of adhesive, create a strong joint. The Kreg Company makes several types of jigs that allow for the quick drilling of pocket holes to attach the pocket screws. For the screws to hold well and the joint to suck tight, a fairly precise angle is needed to ensure you don't split out the wood on the edge. The jigs help ensure the holes drilled for the pocket screws meet these needs and provide uniform strength across the joint. It is particularly useful for case-good construction (the building of cabinets or bookshelves where an outside frame is secured together and then shelving is added within that frame) or building framing units where the outside edges will be seen in the final piece, and you don't want to see exposed screw heads or staples because you are going to stain the piece. We use pocket screws for almost all case goods, particularly bookshelves, so there is some added mechanical fastening to help offset the weight of the objects on the shelves. We sometimes also use the jig to drill holes and inset screws in chair (see Tip #4 in this chapter) or table joints to help strengthen them (Image 1.3).

6 A USEFUL "MODERN" JOINT TECHNIQUE

When building furniture from scratch, we often do not have the time or sometimes the skill to create joints in the ways the old masters did (dovetails, half laps, mortise and tenons, etc.). We want the piece to be secure and provide maximum support and security, as many of the pieces we build are going into stock and will be used for years into the future. We use several "modern" joint methods to speed up

 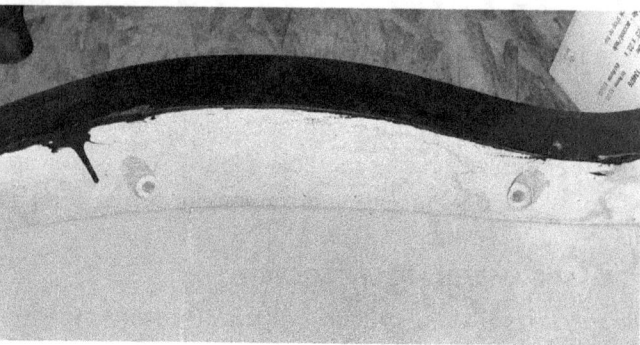

Image 1.3 An illustration showing the angle and drill pattern of a pocket screw in a piece of wood and a photo showing two pocket holes drilled into a framing unit of a table to hold the top on securely.
Source: Illustration and photo by the author.

construction and provide that necessary support. One of these is using glue blocks. The glue block is used chiefly in constructing table tops, chair seat frames, or other flat surfaces framed with a skirt. The glue block is cut at a 45-degree angle and fits in the corner between the two perpendicular framing pieces that frame the skirt of the furniture piece. Glue is applied to all the surfaces and then secured with mechanical fasteners, staples, screws, etc.

Our prop warehouse is very full, so we also often use the glue block to provide a way of securing the legs of the table. That way, we can remove them for storage (saving valuable warehouse space). In this instance, we would attach the glue block in a way that the leg will fit between the skirt and the glue block, or the leg will complete the skirt and the glue block will be placed so it touches the backside of the leg. We then predrill into the glue block one or two locations to allow us to screw or lag bolt on the leg once it is inserted into the table framing. Once the glue blocks have set up, we slide the legs into the framing, attach our screws or lag bolts, and tighten them down. Flip the whole thing over, and we have a table. At the end of the run, we can remove the hardware and slide the legs out of the framing so that the table top is easier to store. We often keep the legs in the tabletop (putting the tabletop into storage face down) so it can all be stored together in very little space, and we can find the legs when we pull the table out to use it in the future (Image 1.4).

Image 1.4 Two photos showing a wooden glue block (left) and a metal glue block (right) being used on table legs.
Source: Photos by the author.

7 CLEANING UP BOLT THREADS

We often run into the issue of having to shorten a bolt or cut down a piece of threaded rod to fit a specific application. In doing the cutting, you can mess up the threads, and it can be nearly impossible to get a nut onto the threads once it has been cut down. We now thread one or two nuts onto the threads on the side we want to keep before cutting the bolt or rod to length. Once we have completed the cut, we then use the nuts to align/rebuild the threads by slowly working them part way off and back onto the threads at the cut; by working them back and forth a few times, we can remove any imperfections and allow the threads to align making the threading on of a nut to be easier and more consistent.

8 POWER CORD MANAGEMENT FOR TOOLS

We have a lot of power tools with cords, and they can become a tangled mess in our tool area, so we tie the cords up so they are more manageable and easier to deal with. (See Image 1.5 for a visual representation of the steps.)

1. We grab the cord and fold it in half.
2. We then half it again (so we have four cord lengths next to each other).

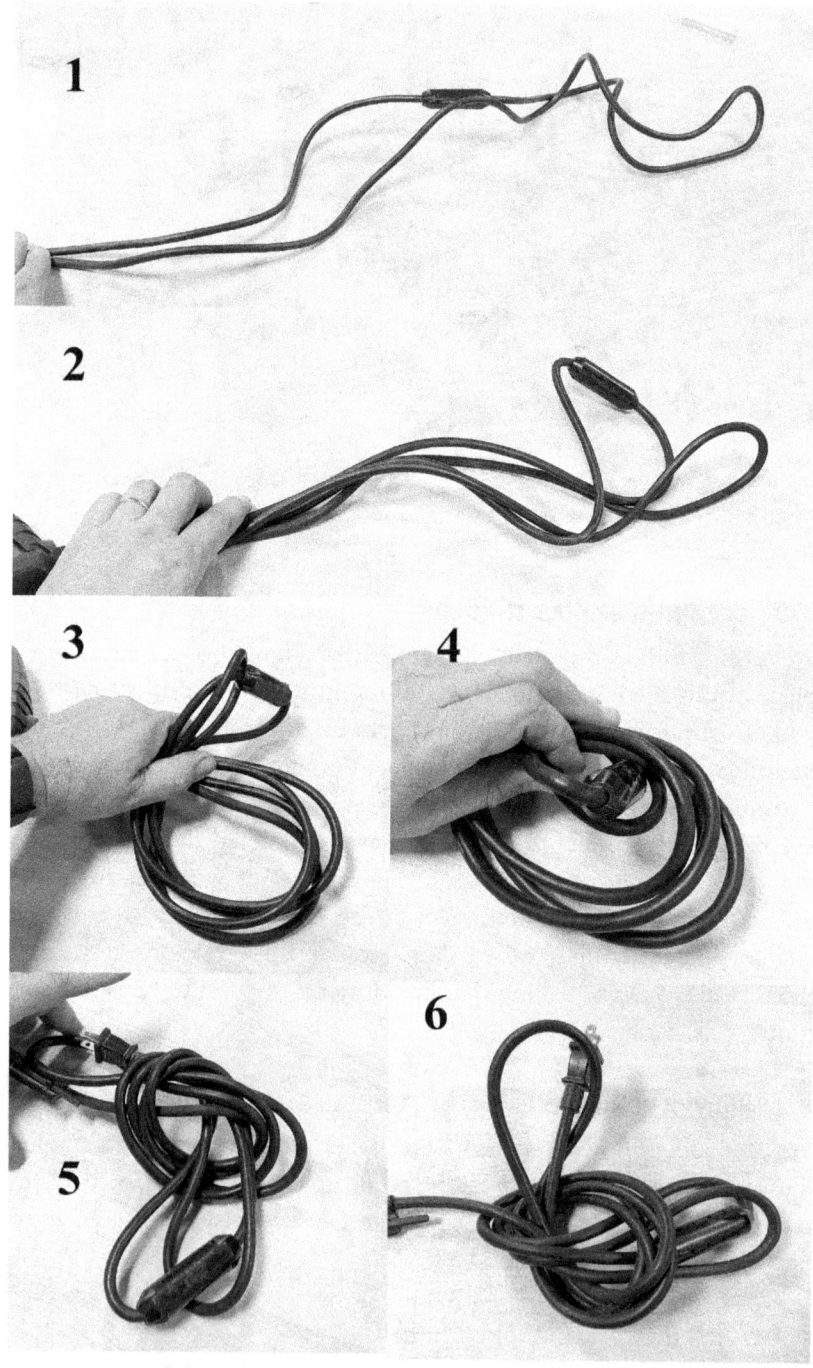

Image 1.5 Photos showing the process we use to tie up our power cords.
Source: Photos by the author.

3. We then create a loop of the four cord lengths.
4. We pass the gathered end through the loop.
5. We then pull it snug.
6. An image of a cord wrapped in the proceeding manner.

It might take a few times of doing this for the cord to learn how it is being folded, but then it will naturally fall into this pattern and be easy to tie up in the future. On some shorter cords, we only half them once and then tie the loop. It releases very easily and keeps the corded tool area much more organized. I have never found this method to be an issue on any of our tools but some people feel this is bad for the cords (particularly the knotting at the end) as it can damage the wires inside the cord. They recommend using Velcro cord straps to hold the cord in its folded state rather than knotting them, which is also a great way to deal with the cord length. Either method will work, so experiment with both and do what works best for you.

9 STRETCH WRAP KEEPS IT TOGETHER

Stretch or cling wrap is an excellent item to have around the shop. It comes in many different widths and also in some colors. The smaller rolls – two inches wide, often come with a dispensing handle to help wrap things. If you are unfamiliar with this material, it is not sticky in and of itself but sticks to itself (it clings), and if you wrap the object tightly, it will do an excellent job of keeping things together. We use it to wrap sets of legs or arms together so similar objects are grouped in our parts bins. We also use it to wrap up sets of casters too big to go into ziplock bags. Much like tape, leaving a courtesy tab on the end of the wrap is a nice thing to do. We do this by leaving a few inches loose, pulling or cutting the wrap off the roll, and then folding over the wrap to create a small double-sided tab. This makes finding the end and unwrapping the items easier than constantly cutting through the wrap.

We also recently cleaned up our floral areas and used it to wrap each type of flower; we gathered all the stems of any kind and color of flower (so all bloomed red roses or white peonies as examples) and then wrapped a few wraps of stretch wrap around the base of the stems. This allows us to store multiple types of flowers in one storage bin, but if you pull out one kind of flower, all of that type of flower will come out together. You can unwrap, pull out what you need, and rewrap them to keep them together (Image 1.6).

Image 1.6 A photo showing stretch wrap securing a group of chair legs together.

Source: Photo by the author.

10 KEEPING YOUR HARDWARE TOGETHER

We often need to take a piece of furniture apart to do repairs or prepare it for new upholstery, and want to keep all the hardware together. Some shops use little magnetic bowls, while others use a press and seal bag (ziplock style). On occasion we use these to, but more often we use our impulse sealer, which is a device to seal plastic bags shut using heat. The nice thing about the impulse sealer is that once you seal the bag, it is nearly impossible for it to pop open and lose a piece of hardware. We put all the hardware for any particular piece of furniture in the bag and then seal it shut add a label to the bag and place it in a safe place so we know all the hardware is safely stored together. It is also great for making ziplock or other storage bags a custom size. We also use it to seal up sets of hardware for installs, or if we send hardware on a rental, we will impulse seal it into bags, so it is much harder for it to get lost in transport. This device/tool is also useful for making blood bags and the like. Ours has a temperature setting dial, so you can adjust it depending on the thickness of the bag you are sealing (Image 1.7).

11 RIGHTY TIGHTY, LEFTY LOOSEY – TURNING THE SCREW OR BOLT THE RIGHT WAY

In most applications, if you turn the object (screw, bolt, etc.) to the right as you are looking at it, it will tighten – righty tighty, and if

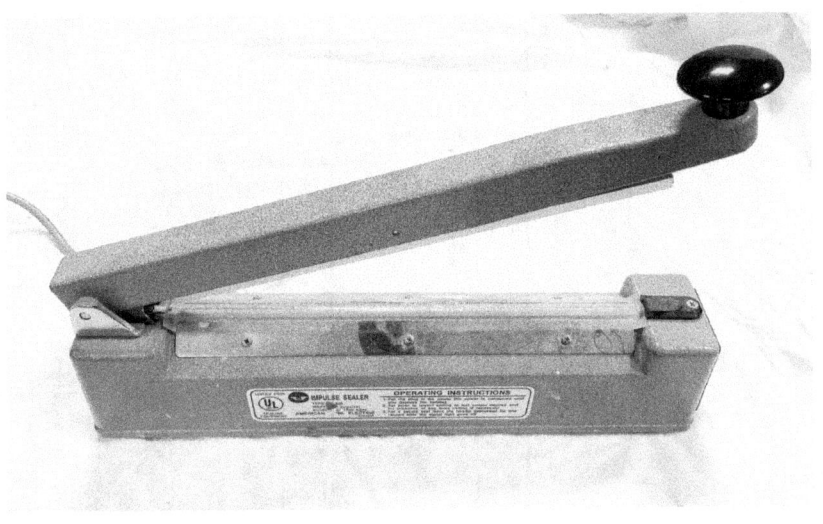

Image 1.7 A photo of an impulse sealer.
Source: Photo by the author.

you turn the same object to the left, it will loosen – lefty loosey. In the old days, we would say clockwise to tighten and counterclockwise to loosen, but so many clocks today are digital that many people don't learn about clock faces. It is even true (and sad) that schools no longer teach kids how to read a traditional clock face to tell time. Save your old clocks; they will become fantastic "period" set dressing in short order.

12 STANDARD FURNITURE DIMENSIONS

Prop people need to know how much space furniture will take up onstage. Here is a list of basic furniture pieces with standard dimensions for each piece. These are not "set in stone" as styles change, but are general sizes for the pieces listed. Knowing these basics will help you in general furniture construction and have a jumping-off point when creating furniture from scratch. Some of the dimensions given are ranges, as sizes vary greatly in that particular type of furniture. Length generally refers to the widest dimension, while width refers to the shorter dimension (often considered depth). Average seat heights are also given for objects that require them. (For metric conversion, multiply the inch measurement by 2.54 to get the number of centimeters.)

12 Carpentry/Basic shop work

	Length	Width	Overall Height	Seat Height
Living Room				
Three seat sofa	84–90" wide	35–38" deep	32"	16–17"
Loveseat	60" wide	35–38" deep	32"	16–17"
Easy chair	25–35" wide	26–38" deep	31"	16–17"
Wingback	30–32" wide	22–25" deep	43"	19"
Coffee table	30–48" long	18–24" wide	19"	n/a
Side/end table	17–24" long	17–24" wide	19–21"	n/a
Sofa table	60–72" long	14" deep	26"	n/a
Dining Room				
Dining table	60–72"	36–40"	29–30"	n/a
Dining chair – armed	18–19"	22–24"	36"	18"
Dining chair – side	18–19"	18–19"	36"	18"
Buffet	54–60"	20–24"	34–38"	n/a
Bedroom				
Twin bed	75–80"	38–39"	6"	n/a
Double/Full bed	75–80"	53–54"	8"	n/a
Queen bed	80"	60"	8"	n/a
King bed	80"	76"	10"	n/a
California King bed	84"	72"	10"	n/a
Night stand	15"–18"	18"–20"	26"	n/a
Low boy dresser	36"	18" deep	36"	n/a
High boy dresser	36"	18" deep	54"	n/a
Chest of drawers	30–42" wide	16–18" deep	44–60"	n/a

Kitchen

Counter	Varies	24–36"	35–36"
Counter stool	12–14"	12–14"	42"
Stove	30" wide	25" deep	36"
Fridge	24–40" wide	29–36" deep	62–72"
Dishwasher	24"	24"	35"
Bar stool	17"	17"	42"
Bar height			40–42"

Counter	24–27"
Counter stool	n/a
Stove	n/a
Fridge	n/a
Dishwasher	n/a
Bar stool	30"
Bar height	28–30"

Home Office

Desk	48"	30"	36"	16–19"
Desk chair	19–22" wide	15–19" deep		

Bathroom

Vanity (single)	30–36" wide	20–23" deep	30–34"	n/a
Toilet	20" wide	27–30" deep	27–32"	17–19"
Bathtub – clawfoot	60" long	33–36"	23"	n/a
Bathtub – inset	52–72" long	30–32"	20–22"	n/a

Misc.

Rocking chair	26"	20"	40"	16"
Card table	36"	36"	30"	n/a
Hall table	55"	15"	27"	n/a
Chaise	73–80"	25–30"	35–40"	15–18"
Ottoman	14–19"	14–19"	16"	n/a
Coat rack	15–19"	15–19"	60–66"	n/a

Carpentry/Basic shop work

Prop math

Two

We use math in prop work every day. Knowing basic math skills is very important to being successful in props. It is important to learn your basic angles, addition, subtraction, and multiplying and dividing; it will come in handy regularly. That said, one of the most valuable pieces of math you can learn is proportional math, which is the comparing of four pieces of information (where you know three of those pieces of information) in fraction form on either side of an equation, which is proportionally equal which you solve to find the missing information. Sometimes, the missing information you want to learn is a percentage of enlargement or reduction you must use on an object to get it to a specific size. This percentage becomes the third piece of information you know, and you are solving for that enlargement or reduction percentage. Tips 13–15 give real-world examples to help make sense of this important but challenging math skill.

13 HOW TO DETERMINE REAL-WORLD SIZES FROM A RESEARCH IMAGE

You are working on a show, and the designer sent a research image of a dining chair they want you to build. They want it to have "standard dimensions," which is all the information they gave when sending in their packet. Luckily, you know standard furniture sizes (or if you don't, you should check out Chapter One, Tip 12). With that information, you know that the standard height for a seat on a dining chair is 18". Knowing that information and having the research photo, you can figure out how tall to make the overall chair. If you take the research image and measure the height of the seat and the height of the overall chair from the floor in the picture, then using proportional math, you can figure out how tall the chair will be in real life. You can see that the measurement of the floor-to-seat height in the photograph is 3", and the chair's overall height is 5.5". Now you know three pieces of

DOI: 10.4324/9781003384182-2

information (both of the dimensions from the research image and the standard seat height in real life) and are searching for a fourth piece (the height of the overall chair in real life). Since you know the photograph of the chair and the actual chair are proportional; you can set up two fractions to determine the height.

With this information, you can create one of your fractions: 3 over 5.5; those are equal (proportionally) to the heights in real life: 18" for the seat and an unknown height for the overall size of the chair, which we will represent with the letter X. These two pieces of information form our second fraction: 18 over X. Since these two fractions are equal you put them on either side of an equal sign and then using math you can figure out the overall height of the chair. Your goal is to solve for X. If you remember back in your middle school math class, you must cross-multiply the fractions to get X multiplied by something on one side of the equation and a number on the other side. Then, you divide by that X multiplier into both sides to determine what X is; that number in inches is the overall height of the chair in real life.

$$\frac{3}{18} = \frac{5.5}{X}$$

Then cross multiple to get

$$99 = 3X$$

Divide both sides by 3 to solve for X.

$$33 = X$$

So, the overall chair height would be 33" tall.

14 ENLARGING AND CROPPING

Our designer found a piece of art that wants to fit into a frame that is 24" wide by 36" high. The designer has told us we can crop the image slightly on the height to make it fit in the frame if needed. The original image they gave us is 6" by 9.5". How much do we need to enlarge the image, and how much, if any, will we end up cropping off the overall height? To answer both questions, we require two separate proportional set-ups. The first is a percentage problem. Since we know the designer wants to maintain the image's width, we will use the 6" as one of our knowns, and we know we want to enlarge it to 24", so those two numbers form the first fraction: 6 over 24. We know we want to enlarge the image and need to know by what percentage we need to do that; since we are enlarging, we will set 100% as equal to the 6" since it is our original size, and we will solve for the percentage we need to increase the image to get it to 24".

The fractions would look like this:

$$\frac{6}{24} = \frac{100}{X}$$

Then cross multiply to get:

$$6X = 2,400$$

Divide both sides by 6 to solve for X.

$$X = 400$$

We need to enlarge the image by 400% to get it to the right size for the frame. How do we determine if we need to crop the image, and by how much? We know the original is 6" by 9.5", and the finished item wants to be 24" by 36"; since the height is in question, we will leave the original height as our unknown to see if we need to crop that 9.5" for the image to remain proportional when we enlarge it by the 400% we just figured out. So, our fractions would be six over unknown (X), which is equal to 24 over 36 (the size in inches of our finished image).

$$\frac{6}{X} = \frac{24}{36}$$

Then cross multiply to get:

$$24X = 216$$

Divide both sides by 24 to solve for X.

$$X = 9$$

Since the original image we were given was 9.5" tall, we will need to crop ½ an inch off the original image's height and then enlarge it by 400% to fit in the frame.

15 HOW TO DETERMINE THE PERCENTAGE INCREASE OR DECREASE OF PAPER PROPS

To increase or decrease a paper prop (ephemera) on a copier is often done in props; many people keep trying different settings until they get to the desired size, but there is a different and better method that allows you to hit on the exact enlargement or reduction size without guessing. A proportional math formula like the above one also works in this situation. We have a vintage frame that is a unique size 7½" by 12½", and we want to put a photo of a soldier into that frame for a production of *The Glass Menagerie*. The picture of the soldier we located is currently 3" by 5". We must set up proportions to determine the percentage to increase the image to fit in the frame. The first one is the current size over the desired size. Then, since we need to know how large to make it, we will establish our second fraction as our starting size of 100% over our unknown enlargement percentage.

$$\frac{3}{7.5} = \frac{100}{X}$$

Then cross-multiply.

$$3X = 750$$

Divide both sides by 3 to solve for X.

$$X = 250$$

We would enlarge the original photo to 250% of its original size, and it would fit in the frame.

To verify that this works, we can check the other original dimension in the same way:

$$\frac{5}{12.5} = \frac{100}{X}$$

Cross-multiply to get

$$5X = 1,250$$

Divide by 5 to get

$$X = 250$$

This verifies that our math is correct, and if we enlarge by 250%, the image will fit into the frame.

The same idea would be used to determine reducing the size of an image. We are creating a passport for *The 39 Steps*. The designer found an image of the front of a passport they liked and sent it to us. When we opened it in Adobe Photoshop, the picture they sent was 11" tall by about 7-3/4" wide. We researched and found that a standard passport is generally 4.92" in height by 3.46" in width. To determine the percentage, we had to shrink the passport image to make it the correct size, so we set up a proportion. With the size of the current image (11) over the size, we want it to be (4.92) as our first fraction. Knowing that the image is currently 11", we can set up our percentage fraction with the current size (100%) over our unknown percentage (X).

$$\frac{11}{4.92} = \frac{100}{X}$$

We then cross-multiply

$$492 = 11X$$

Then Divide by 11 to get X alone.

$$X = 44.73\%$$

So, we can use the image size feature in Adobe Photoshop or whatever graphics program you use, set the attribute to percentage mode, and enter 44.73 in the box. Once we do that, we hit return, and the image will be resized to the correct size for use on the passport. If we check the math here by doing the other dimensions, we will find the percentage to be 44.65%, which is nearly identical. We could choose a number in the middle, 44.69 or 44.7, to balance as much as possible.

16 ADDING FRACTIONS

Adding fractions can be frustrating if you don't know what you are doing. You are looking for a common denominator. So, if you are trying to add ¼", 1/8", and 1/16", then you would use the largest number (16) as the common denominator. So, to get ¼" to 16" you would multiply both the bottom and top number by 4 giving you 4/16", to get 1/8" there you would multiple by 2 giving you 2/16", then you would add all three numbers together: 4/16ths, 2/16ths and 1/16th, and would end up with 7/16ths. After adding, you may find that the numbers are divisible, and you can do that to get to a more manageable number. For instance, if you ended up with 10/16ths after adding your fractions, that is divisible by 2, giving you 5/8ths.

Sometimes, the fractions you want to add together need denominators that are easy to determine a common number for. In this case, I recommend multiplying the denominators to find a number that works as a common denominator. Then, once the addition is done, you can see if there is a number you can divide the numerator and denominator by to reduce the fraction. As an example, adding 2/3rds and ¼. You would need to multiply these fractions to get a common denominator of 12. For the first fraction, multiply by 4 to get 8/12ths, and the second you would multiply by three to get 3/12ths. When added together you get 11/12ths, which is not reduceable, so the addition of those fractions would result in a new fraction: 11/12ths.

17 BE VERY AWARE OF YOUR UNITS OF MEASUREMENT

When looking at drawings or information from designers, stage management, directors, etc., be aware of the unit(s) of measure. Try to be consistent when sharing that information; don't have one measurement in inches and another in feet and inches on the same drawing. Take a minute to consider the size of the object you are representing in your drawing and if it makes more sense to use inches or if feet and inches make more sense, and then make sure you are consistent as you dimension out your drawing. Many measurements are very close in size and can be misleading, such as 34" and 3'–4" (a difference of 6") or 48" and 4'–8" (a difference of 8"). So being consistent in how you dimension things can help reduce that confusion. It also helps to make a note on the drawing, something to the effect of: "all measurements are given in inches" as an example. Always double-check measurements and make sure they make sense before you begin cutting.

Units of measure can be particularly tricky if you are working with a designer from another country that uses a different base system of measurement than you are used to. Early in my career, I was working on a production of *The Wizard of OZ* at a theater here in the United States, while the designer was from Great Britain. So, when the drawings arrived, everything was dimensioned in Metric. We, luckily, noticed reasonably quickly and spent about two days converting all the dimensions to Imperial measurements. Before we built anything, we also verified the sizes of things with the technical director as many of the smaller prop units needed to fit through "doors" (really giant hinged panels in the Cyc) built into the set, so we wanted to verify that they had converted all the measurements correctly so that the units we were building would fit through the openings.

18 CONVERTING TO A SINGLE UNIT OF MEASUREMENT

Sometimes, it is easier or more convenient for the math to convert everything to inches (or centimeters) to figure something out. In our recent production of *The Play That Goes Wrong*, our designer sent in the drawing of the window unit with measurements up the side denoting baseboard height (6"), baseboard to the bottom of window trim (1'–5"), the width of window trim (5"), the height of the window (6'–3"), the width of top window trim (5"), top of window trim to crown molding (2'–4"), and width of crown molding (1'–6"). He also included an overall wall height. I needed to make curtains for the windows that lived in a valance that was placed just above the window molding and was 1'–0" tall. The curtains were supposed to be centered in that valance and hang below the window frame by 6". To figure out the height of the curtains, I needed to add up the multiple dimensions he had listed, which were in both feet and inches.

Width of lower window trim + height of window + width of upper window trim + length of curtain hidden in valance + length of curtain below window frame

$$5" + 6'-5" + 5" + 6" + 6"$$

I then converted all the dimensions to inches and added them all up.

$$5" + 77" + 5" + 6" + 6" = 99"$$

Once I had the total number of inches, I divided by 12 to get the number of feet.

$$99/12 = 8.25$$

In that division, I ended up with a remainder of .25. That represents the portion of a foot (the number of inches) that remains. By multiplying that decimal by 12, I get 3. This means the curtain needs to be 8 feet 3 inches long.

Make sure that when you convert back to feet and inches, you know the steps so things don't get off. You divide the total number of inches by 12 to get the number of feet, then take whatever decimal remainder you have and multiply that by 12 to determine the number of inches. Sometimes, you will end up with a decimal at that point, which is the parts of an inch left over .125 = 1/8th", .25 = ¼", etc. Something similar could be done with metric and it would be easier in many ways. You generally move the decimal point to the left or right as you convert between centimeters, decimeters, and meters.

19 MEASUREMENT TOLERANCES WHEN BUILDING FURNITURE WITH MOVING PARTS

When building a piece of furniture that has moving parts, make sure to give yourself a bit of a gap to allow for doors and drawers to move freely; we typically provide 1/16" of an inch on each side of the drawer or door (so 1/8" total overall on height and width). This allows the moving parts to swing or move freely but not so much gap that they look bad or fit poorly.

20 DON'T GET TOO PRECISE IN YOUR MEASURING

When working with small measurements, don't go beyond 1/16"; it is not noticeable and will save you tons of headaches. If you are trying to measure a 32nd or smaller, the width of your writing utensil alone could throw you off. It will not be noticeable, and the time you spend working on the math could be better spent building the object. On most items, I would recommend working with 1/8ths, only getting into 1/16ths if the level of detail is super fine or the prop/object will be filmed in high definition for a film or movie production. The only exception might be if you are working on an effect system or a mechanical movement, and more precision might be necessary. However, if you are getting that precise for theater, it might backfire on you. Often, the visual look and proportion of the object is more important than the exact measurement.

That being said, I once worked with a designer who carried a tape measure with them all the time, and they would often pull it out and measure spacings to see if we had followed the drawing exactly. On one particular unit, we adjusted the drawer heights to allow them to move easily (see Tip #19 in this chapter), and he got angry that we had not followed his dimensions on the drawing. I had to explain that the overall cabinet size could not be made larger due to the space onstage. He had not given us any tolerance in the drawing to allow for drawer movement, so we reduced the size of the drawers by 1/8" in each direction to allow the drawers to open and close. He was not happy that we had "modified" his design. Still, the piece of furniture looked correct on stage, and it functioned for the performers, both of which were more important than the actual size of the drawer.

21 BASIC INFORMATION ABOUT ANGLES

Angles and arcs are handy in props, and knowing how to work with them can be super beneficial – here are a few useful angles to always keep in mind. Ninety degrees is a right angle, or the equivalent of a perfectly square corner cut. One hundred eighty degrees is a straight line. A 45-degree angle is a miter corner like you would find on a picture frame. Imagine cutting a square from corner to corner to get two equilateral triangles; that angle is 45 degrees. Often, when cutting an angle in a piece of wood, you need to consider whether you need the angle the saw is set to or its opposite, whether it is an inside or an outside cut. Take a minute to think about which side you need before making that slice so that your blade width is cut on the right side of the line and you don't end up with a piece that is too short or long (Image 2.1).

22 CUTTING ANGLES IN MOLDING

When working with angles in molding, you need to know how to cut the pieces so they fit together tightly. You do this by bisecting the angle (dividing it in half) and creating even pieces so the lengths of the ends of the boards line up. If you fit two pieces of molding around a

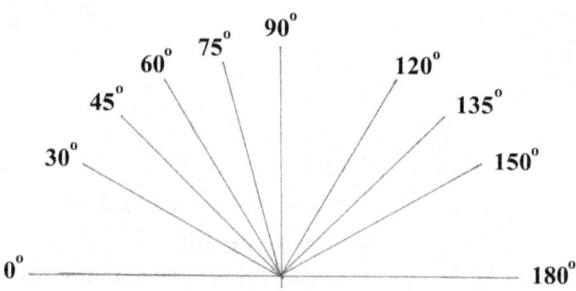

Image 2.1 An illustration of basic angles.
Source: Illustration by the author.

90-degree corner on a cabinet, you would divide that angle in half and get 45 degrees. So, you would need to cut corresponding 45-degree angles in both pieces of wood so that when they come together, they fit tightly and close up the entire 90-degree angle of the piece you are putting the molding on. This, of course, can get trickier when the angles are not 90 degrees. But know that if you cut both sides to the same degrees, they should line up correctly. If dealing with an eight-sided (octagonal) shape, your cuts would all be 22.5 degrees on each piece because the total angle would be 45 degrees. With a six-sided figure, each cut would be 30 degrees; each angle would need to total 60 degrees. This method of bisecting (cutting two halves) will work for any angle you are trying to make line up exactly. If this needs to be clarified, I suggest taking a piece of molding and cutting a 30-degree cut and a 60-degree cut to see how they would line up (or not) to create a 90-degree corner.

Soft goods/Sewing

Three

Sewing is another crucial aspect of props; unlike costumes, which deal mainly with clothing, props deals with many different types of fabric items, from bedding and curtains to puppets and banners and a host of other things. Soft goods is a term that refers to any prop item that is fabric-based (soft) as compared to steel or wood (hard); it encompasses many items like those listed above and a host of other items. Basic hand sewing and machine sewing skills are a great basic skill set to have. As you advance in your career more specialized and detailed sewing skills will be acquired. Here are some tips and tricks that will help on many fabric projects.

23 THE BEST SEAM CLOSING STITCH

One of the most common hand-stitching efforts we do is to close up the final edge of a pillow. I cannot count the number of pillows I have made over the years. On occasion, adding a zipper to a pillow to remove the cover is helpful. In most productions you don't want to see that zipper, so we hand-stitch our pillows closed to give them nice, clean edges. To do this we use a stitch that I have heard referred to by many names, including the ladder, the princess, the blind stitch, or the Henson stitch. When we are done, it is often nearly impossible to figure out which side of the pillow was hand-stitched closed and which was sewn by the sewing machine.

This stitch requires folding over the fabric on both sides of the seam, creating a narrow hem, much like when sewing a seam on the sewing machine. (See Image 3.1 for a visual representation of how to sew this stitch.) You thread your needle with a color of thread that coordinates with your pillow and knot the end. Start on the inside of one of those folds (hem) and run the needle out from inside the seam. You then go directly across into the other fold and insert your needle; you run the needle along the fold a short distance (1/8"),

The ladder stitch illustrated

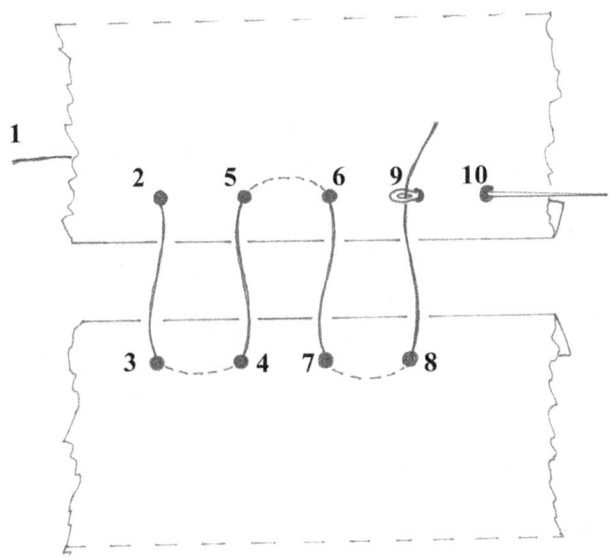

Image 3.1 An illustration showing the steps to the ladder stitch.
Source: Illustration by the author.

pop the needle out of the fabric, go directly across into the other fold, and repeat the process, creating a zipper-like pattern of back and forth stitches. As you do this, you snug up each stitch, and the seam begins to close up. You can use smaller or larger stitches depending on how tight you want the seam to be.

One other great thing about this stitch is that if your sewing of the piece was a bit off and you have a bit more fabric on one side of the seam than the other, you can cheat the cross stitching slightly forward to pull the fabric a little at a time into the seam, so when you get to the end of the seam you don't have a chunk of fabric on one side that is left over, but it is spread out throughout the seam and once tightened will mostly disappear.

24 TURNING OUT TUBES OF FABRIC

Occasionally, you need to make a narrow fabric tube, either for a strap on a traveling pack or maybe for a chandelier sock (a fabric tube used to cover the electrical cord and hanging hardware for a chandelier). Once the tube is sewn, you must turn the tube right side out. We have two main methods to do this. A fabric turner tool can slide through

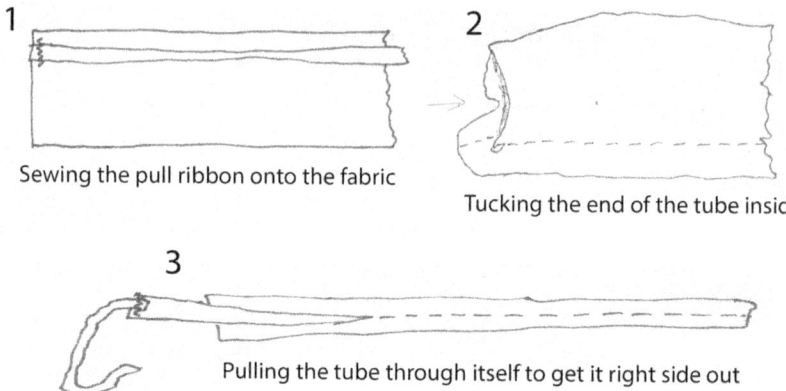

Image 3.2 Illustrations showing a method for turning tubes of fabric right side out after sewing.
Source: Illustrations by the author.

your tube, hook into the other side, and help pull it right side out. This works well for short tubes and slick fabrics but can snag or bog down when dealing with long tubes or clingy fabrics. (See Image 3.2 for a visual reference to the steps in this process.) In these instances, we often sew a piece of tie-line or a strong narrow ribbon into one end of the fabric we are turning into a tube (1). We then run the ribbon or tie-line the length of the future tube leaving it sticking out the other end by a few inches. Then you sew the piece of fabric into the tube, making sure to not sew over the tie-line or ribbon. Once you are done sewing, you feed the end of the tube that has the ribbon/tie-line attached into the tube slightly (2). Grab a second person and have them hold the tube and work the fabric with you, you can pull on the ribbon/tie-line, and slowly work the fabric through the tube turning it right side out (3). Be careful and go slow; you don't want the fabric to bunch up on itself and become nearly impossible to pull through or to rip out your ribbon/tie-line. This is likely to occur if the tube gets too small/tight.

25 VELCRO AND SNAP TAPE FOR QUICK RELEASING OF ITEMS

Being a Shakespeare festival, we use a lot of banners, many of which need to appear in one scene and then disappear in the next. We often want actors to rip down these banners on stage, but we need them to last for multiple performances. We rely on two methods to do this successfully: Velcro or snap tape. Velcro creates a great ripping sound but can be hard to remove if the banner is long (tall) and the actor mostly pulls straight down. In these instances, we tend to use snap tape.

Snap tape is a piece of twill tape with snaps (pin snap connections on one side and socket snap connections on the other) attached at evenly spaced intervals along it. We sew one side of the snap tape to the banner, and the other connects to the structure holding the banner. We often have a steel or wood structure to which the banner is attached, in which case we would staple or screw the corresponding piece of snap tape to the rigid structure. To secure the banner, you snap the corresponding parts together. With some slight pressure (a pull), the snaps begin to pop apart and the banner falls. We have found that banners of different weights require different numbers of snaps to be connected, so experimenting with how many snaps you secure will be critical to a successful "rip" (Image 3.3).

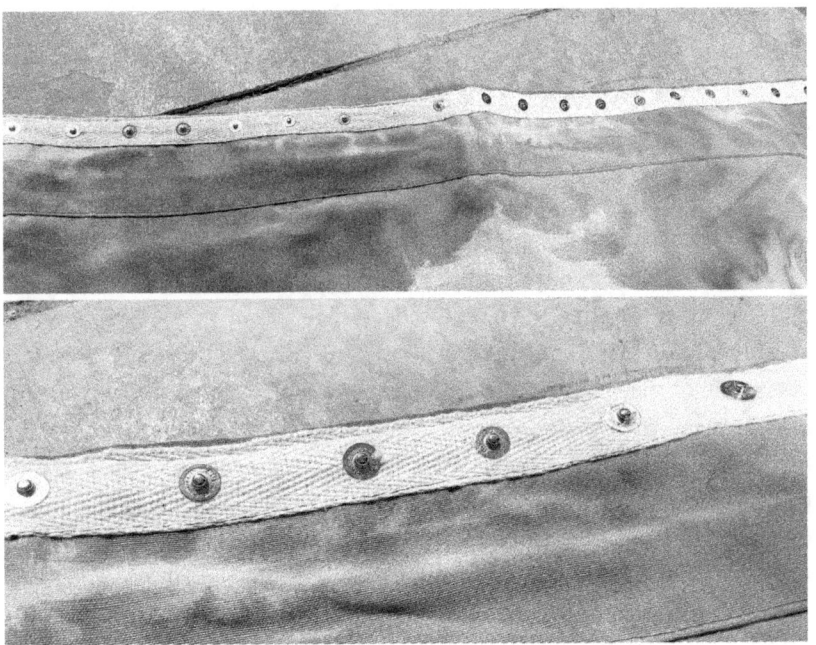

Image 3.3 Photos showing snap tape being used on a banner. Further away view (top), close up of snaps (lower).

Source: Photos by the author.

26 WAYS OF MARKING FABRIC

There are many ways to mark fabric before cutting or sewing it, and you should consider how the fabric is being used or how it will be seen onstage to determine the best method. You can use a pencil or a marker; chalk is an excellent way to mark fabric, but on some colors of fabric, it won't dust off easily (mainly the blue chalk). Not only are there chalk blocks, but there are also chalk rollers. There are also several types of marking pens; some are air dispersant (if you leave them exposed to air for a while, the marks will disappear), and others require you to wash the fabric (this won't work on all the fabric types as some are not washable). Recently, we have found some fabric markers and pencils whose marks disappear with the addition of heat (an iron!). Again, this won't work on all fabrics, but knowing the existing options will allow you to mark the fabric as you need to do the project and remove the markings before the prop is finished.

27 SEWING MACHINE FEET YOU SHOULD KNOW

We use a lot of different feet for specific tasks. You should be familiar with and know how to use three in particular. (They will save you so much time.) The first one is the zipper or cording foot; this foot has only one forward leg that rests on the fabric. This allows the needle to get closer to the edge of the fabric (think narrower hem) or to a zipper or cording, which makes for a tighter and more polished-looking seam. Second is the free-hand foot (see Image 3.4), which holds the fabric down like other feet but allows you to move the fabric in multiple directions much more easily. It is excellent for quilting projects or free-form embroidery-type work.

The third foot is the roll hem foot (see Image 3.5), this one will take a bit of getting used to. You twist the fabric into the front of the foot and, as you begin to sew, it curls the fabric's edge into a tight three layers and feed those layers under the needle to create a tiny three-layered hem on the fabric. This works best with thinner, more delicate fabrics (where you would probably not want a super wide seam or edge seam because it would weigh down the fabric and create a visually thick edge). It works very well on silks, satins, and the like. We almost always use a roll hem foot for flags and lightweight banners as It gives them a nice clean edge with little bulk, and they won't fray as easily. These feet come in different sizes that create different widths of hem, so make sure you know what size you are buying.

Image 3.4 A photo of a free-hand foot on a sewing machine.
Source: Photo by the author.

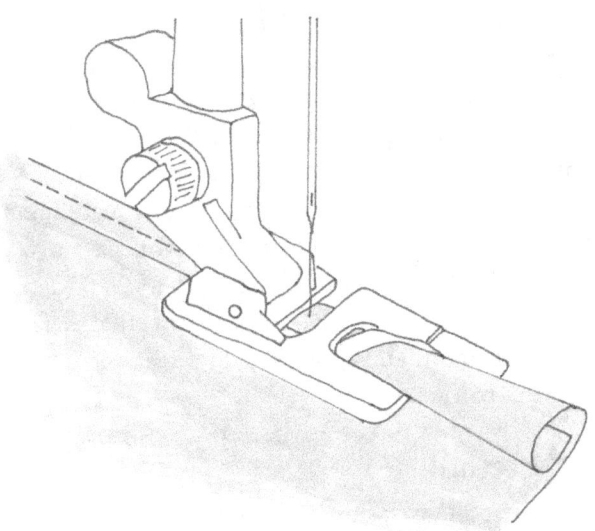

Image 3.5 An illustration showing the roll hem foot and how it rolls and hems the edge of the fabric.
Source: Illustration by the author.

28 CREATING A SPHERE OF FABRIC

Sometimes, we are asked to make something that is just a bit bizarre. For a preshow event a few years back, we were asked to make a catapult to launch sheep into the audience. After working through the logistics, we realized the sheep should be spherical to fit the catapult and launch nicely into the audience. We bought some large kickballs and needed to cover them in faux sheep fur. We measured the circumference of the balls, and divided that number in half to determine the size we needed to make our pattern pieces. We used the sphere pattern piece (see Image 3.6) and enlarged it so that the length of the inner shape was equal to half the circumference of the balls we were trying to cover. This pattern has a built-in seam allowance which will get larger as you enlarge the pattern so be sure to mark it well on the fabric to ensure that your fabric cover will fit your ball snugly. You can use the proportional math tip (Chapter Two, Tip 16) to determine the size of enlargement or reduction you need. Once you have the correct size of the pattern, you then need to cut out six of that shape from your fabric(s). Sew three together to make roughly a circle, and press all your seams flat. You might need to snip some of your seam allowance to allow the curves to lay flat. Repeat with the other three pieces, and similarly press the seams. Then, place the two three-panel pieces faces together and sew them most of the way together, pressing the seam and trimming, or snipping, where needed. Then flip your entire sphere right side out and stuff it with your preferred filling. Once stuffed to your desired firmness, hand stitch the small opening closed (see Tip #23 earlier in this chapter). Now you have a fabric sphere. In our case we had to fit the fabric sphere around our kickballs so we sewed the two half-spheres only half way together, wrapped them around the kickball and then using the ladder stitch hand sewed them closed around the ball.

29 SPIKING A TABLECLOTH

We have often found that an actor needs to set a tablecloth or runner on a table onstage as part of the action; invariably, they get the tablecloth crooked, and it looks terrible throughout the scene. Our most straightforward solution to this problem is to sew some spikes into the fabric so that if the actor lines up the spikes with the edges of the table, the cloth will be on the table straight and even. The easiest way for

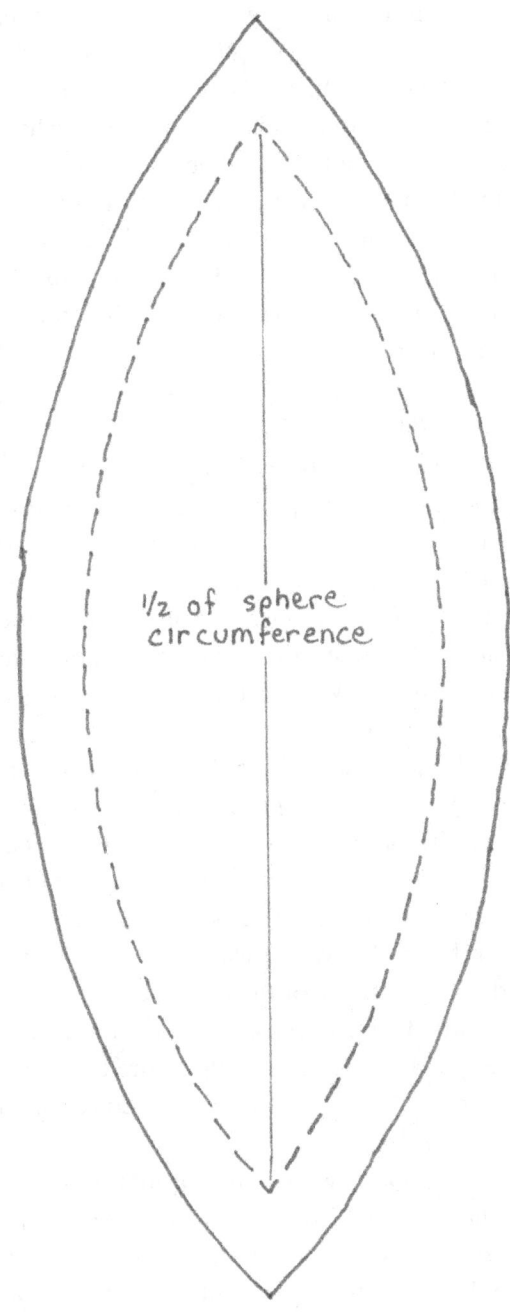

Image 3.6 An illustration of the sphere pattern.
Source: Illustration by the author.

us to do this is to place the cloth or runner on the table in its correct orientation and then mark (with pins or with a heat erasable marker) the table's edges through the fabric. Once that is done, we take the cloth to the sewing machine and do one-inch long zig-zag stitches in a color that blends with the color(s) of the fabric but is also noticeable by the performer along the lines of the corners that we marked. They just need to line up those marks with the table, and voila, a perfectly placed tablecloth. This works particularly well with a round table and four spikes, allowing for the cloth to sit centered on the table and hang off an even amount all the way around.

30 PERFECTLY PROPORTIONED ANIMAL SCULPTURES

Another thing we have found we have been doing more of recently is creating three-dimensional soft sculpture animals for various productions; two that come to mind are the full-size wild hog at the beginning of *Big River* that Huck Finn has to cut the head off of and sprinkle the blood around the cabin so it looks as if he has been killed, and also the royal deer that is killed offstage and then carried on lashed to a stick in William Shakespeare's *As you Like it*. It can be challenging and time-consuming to figure out the patterning of these animals to make their proportions work and make them look realistic/believable.

A few years back, we had a breakthrough that has made this process so much easier. Many stuffed animal companies make very lifelike animal replicas on a small scale. We do some research and find the animal that looks proportionally the best and is closest to what we ultimately want to build in full scale. We purchase the stuffed animal and then take photos and measurements of the toy. Once that is complete, we disassemble the stuffed animal, separating each piece. As we do this, we label every piece and, depending on the complexity of the stuffed animal, might print out some of the photos and add comments and notes to the images and labels.

Once the animal is entirely apart, we use the proportional math problem (presented in Chapter Two, Tip 15) to determine the percentage of increase we would need to apply to our pieces to enlarge them to a life-size scale. We scan the pieces into a computer and then import them into a graphics program (we tend to use Adobe Photoshop, but other options exist). Once in a graphic program, we use the scaling feature to increase the size of our pattern pieces by the percentage we have determined we need. Once enlarged, we print them out as patterns on cheap paper on our large format printer (Chapter Seven, Tip 71).

We then lay out the patterns on fabric or faux fur depending on what would work best for the creature we are trying to reproduce (making sure we are laying out the correct side of the pattern on the right side of the fabric). You don't want all the fur on the inside of the deer! Then, we cut out the pieces and sew them together using the original photos as our guide. Depending on the complexity of the animal, we sometimes find we need to stuff some parts as we go. Also, we sometimes discover we need to add some internal structure (a skeleton) to allow it to move in a realistic fashion. Once it is all sewn up and stuffed sufficiently, we do some hand sewing of the final few joints, and then we have a life-size animal that should be proportionate to the small stuffed animal we purchased at the beginning of the project.

Upholstery/Drapery

Four

Nearly every show has some form of drapery or upholstered items in it, so having a firm grasp of the skills needed in these areas will serve you well. Understanding the traditional methods of both of these skills is helpful, but understanding that the way we use these items on stage varies significantly from how they would be used in a real-world setting. We often modify the methods to fit our budget, time, and show needs. The amount of furniture that actors stand on in plays that they would never stand on in real life is noteworthy. We reinforce most of our upholstered furniture with plywood bases (removing springs) so they are more stable for standing on. Also true with draperies, we often use a quick staple method (Tip #35) to give the look of pleated curtains without spending hours in the soft goods room sewing the pleats into the fabric. The look is the same, and the amount of time saved aids us in completing other projects for the show.

31   HOW MUCH PIPING WRAP YOU CAN GET FROM A SPECIFIC PIECE OF FABRIC

Bias tape has many uses and names; for this chapter, I will call it piping wrap, as that is how we generally use it. We create piping wrap to wrap around cording to create edge detail for upholstery projects. While you can buy bias tape at craft, fabric, and big box stores, it generally won't match the fabric your designer has chosen for the upholstery project. Making piping wrap using the upholstery fabric so it matches the rest of the upholstery gives a more professional and polished look to the finished project. There are three different formulas we use to determine piping wrap needs. Each uses different information to give you the necessary answer, so see which one fits your information and use it to determine your solution. As I mentioned in Chapter Two, Tip 23, you should convert all your measurements when doing these formulas to inches, and then, if you need to, in the end, you can convert them back to feet. I recommend adding 10%–15% to your numbers for waste when determining the length of piping wrap you need. Due to the nature of cutting and trimming, you will end up with some lengths toward the end of your project that wouldn't be the right size, so having a little extra will keep you from having to make more piping wrap later. (To convert these formulas to metric you would multiply the inch measurement by 2.54 to get the number of centimeters.)

a. This formula calculates how many yards of fabric you need to get a predetermined length of piping wrap of a certain width. You start by multiplying the length of the amount of bias tape or piping wrap you need (in inches) by the width (in inches) you want your bias tape or piping wrap to be when it is complete. This determines the number of square inches of fabric you will need. Then, divide that number by the width of the fabric (in inches), not including the selvage edge. You will arrive at the number of linear inches of fabric needed to get that amount of piping wrap. You divide that number by 36 to determine the number of yards of fabric required. Written out the formula looks like this:

Length of wrap needed × width of wrap = square inches needed / fabric width = fabric needed in inches / 36 = yards required.

For 100 feet of piping wrap 2" wide from a 54" wide upholstery fabric, the formula would look like this:

1,200" × 2" = 2,400" / 54" = 44" / 36 = 1.235, or roughly one and a quarter yard of fabric would be needed.

b. This formula determines how big of a square of fabric you need to get the amount of piping wrap you need. Once again, you will need to know the length of the amount of piping wrap you need (in inches) as well as the width you desire. You multiply those two numbers to get the total square inches required. Then, take the square root of that number and round up to the nearest whole number. This number is the number of inches each side of your square needs to be to get the amount of piping wrap out of it. Written out the formula looks like this:

Length of wrap needed × width of wrap = square inches needed / square root = length of each side of the square of fabric needed to get that amount of piping wrap (rounded up to the next whole number).

Using the same information from above the formula math would look like this:

1,200" × 2" = 2,400" / square root = 48.99, or a square that is 50" by 50" would produce that amount of piping wrap.

c. This third formula tells you how much piping wrap of a certain width a piece of fabric of a specific size will yield. You start by measuring the length of the fabric (minus ½" seam allowance) and multiply that by the width of the fabric (minus ½" seam allowance); you divide that by the width of the wrap you are trying to make. The number you come out with is the length (in inches) of the amount of piping wrap that piece of fabric will yield. Written out, the formula looks like this:

(Length of fabric − ½") × (width of fabric − ½") = square inches available/width of wrap = number of inches of length of wrap that material will produce

For a piece of fabric 1-yard square, the formula would look like this: 35.5" × 35.5" = 1,260.25/2" = 630" of linear wrap, or just over 52'.

32   TURN A PIECE OF FABRIC INTO A CONTINUOUS PIECE OF PIPING WRAP

Some people cut diagonal strips of fabric and sew them together individually to get a longer piece of piping wrap. While I appreciate the simple nature of this system, I stumbled across a description years ago of a way to do a few steps and create a very long single piece of piping wrap. It is a more time-effective method of producing this item. Two steps in this process are a bit tricky, but once you get the hang of it, this will save you time and energy in making long lengths of piping wrap. We use a 1/2' seam allowance on this project. (See Image 4.1 for visual reference of some of the steps in this process – numbered below.)

1. To begin creating piping wrap from a single piece of fabric, you need to determine the size of the fabric you need; it should be a square, which will work best for this method of piping wrap construction – using one of the formulas from Tip #33 in this chapter determine the size of your fabric square.

2. Then, lay the fabric square out with the front of the fabric up on a smooth, flat surface. You will want to have already determined the width of your piping wrap in the formula. We typically use a 2" width as that is wide enough to allow for different sizes of cording to be sewn into it and gives you a decent amount of flange left to sew into the cushion or pillow or to staple to the furniture frame. It also happens to be the width of most of our long rulers, making the layout easier.
3. You then draw diagonal lines (45 degrees to the edge of the square) (starting at the points of the fabric) in parallel across the entire length/width of the fabric. The lines should be the width of your finished piping wrap, as determined in step 2. (See Image 4.1 Image 1.)
4. Once that is done, you turn the fabric into a tube (right side in), aligning the lines on the edge as best you can. This is one of the tricky parts as you need to offset the fabric slightly (the width of your seam allowance) so that when you sew the tube the drawn lines line up. Pin along the seam turning your square of fabric into a tube shape.
5. Once that tube is pinned together, you sew along the line of pins.
6. Iron the seam allowance flat, spreading it to both sides, and flip the fabric right side out.
7. Then, you choose one line and cut along it from the left side to the right side. This will give you a parallelogram with lines parallel to the longer sides on it. (See Image 4.1 Image 2.).
8. Now, the trickiest part. You want to align the lines again like in step 4 but this time offset by one row to the right. Take one point of the parallelogram and match it to the other end of its own line, then move it one line over and pin it — again with the right side in. (See Image 4.1 Image 3.) Keep in mind to overlap by the seam allowance as before so the line is straight after it is sewn together. It feels like you are twisting the fabric around into an unhappy shape, and depending on the weight of the fabric and the size of your square, it can be a bit cumbersome.
9. Once pinned along the length, sew along that line of pins and press the seam allowance flat out to both sides.
10. Turn your slightly offset tube right side out.
11. Then, you take a pair of scissors and begin cutting on your line at one end of the fabric roll. (See Image 4.1 Image 4.) If you have

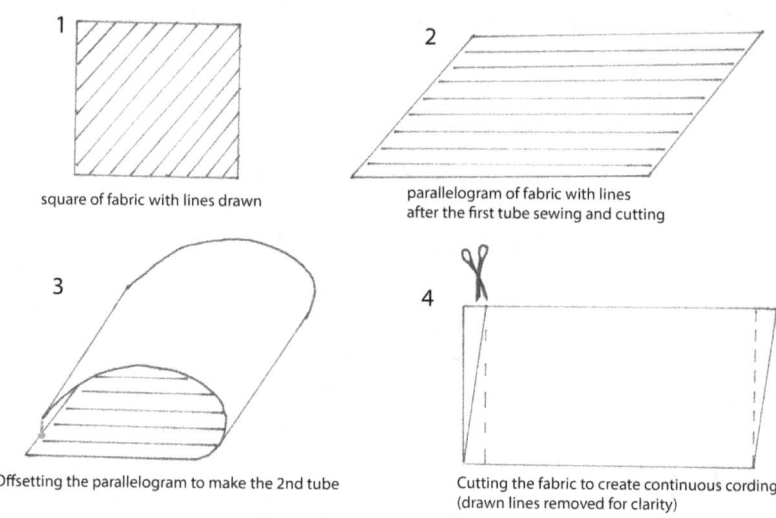

Image 4.1 Illustrations showing the steps in turning a square of fabric into a continuous length of piping wrap.
Source: Illustrations by the author.

done it correctly, you will have created a continuous strip of fabric that is cut on the bias to be used for the piping of your furniture piece or as bias tape for a multitude of projects. Sometimes the lines do not match exactly, but that is okay; split the difference with your scissors. The lines will end up at the outer edge of your bias tape, or the piping wrap and will get sewn into the project and will not be seen.

33 DETERMINING PERCENTAGE FULLNESS FOR DRAPES AND CURTAINS

This needs some clarification, as some designers call a flat panel 100% fullness, while others look at that as 0% fullness. I live in the latter camp and believe that if the fabric is lying flat, it has no fullness, so refer to it as 0%; one of the leading theatrical drapery manufacturers also refers to a flat panel as 0% fullness. Before beginning a drapery project verify that you and the designer are on the same page about this before you figure out how much fabric you need. We will use a 36" wide curtain panel as an example. 0% fullness means there are no pleats, fullness, or gathering of any kind; the fabric is flat, so the curtain panel would be 36" wide and use 36" of fabric. If the designer asks for 25% fullness, you will use a quarter more fabric (in this instance, 9"). The curtain would be 36" wide but use 45" of fabric. If the designer asks for 50% fullness, you will use the 36" plus half as much again, or 18" more. The curtain would be 36" wide but use 54" of Fabric. If the designer asks for 100% fullness, you would double the amount of fabric so the curtain would be 36" wide but use 72" of fabric.

34 DIFFERENT STYLES OF DRAPERY

Drapery comes in many styles. Over the course of my career I have dealt with all the versions shown here as well as some weird combinations of them as well. I choose the most common ones and did illustrations of them in both plan view and front view. (See Image 4.2.)

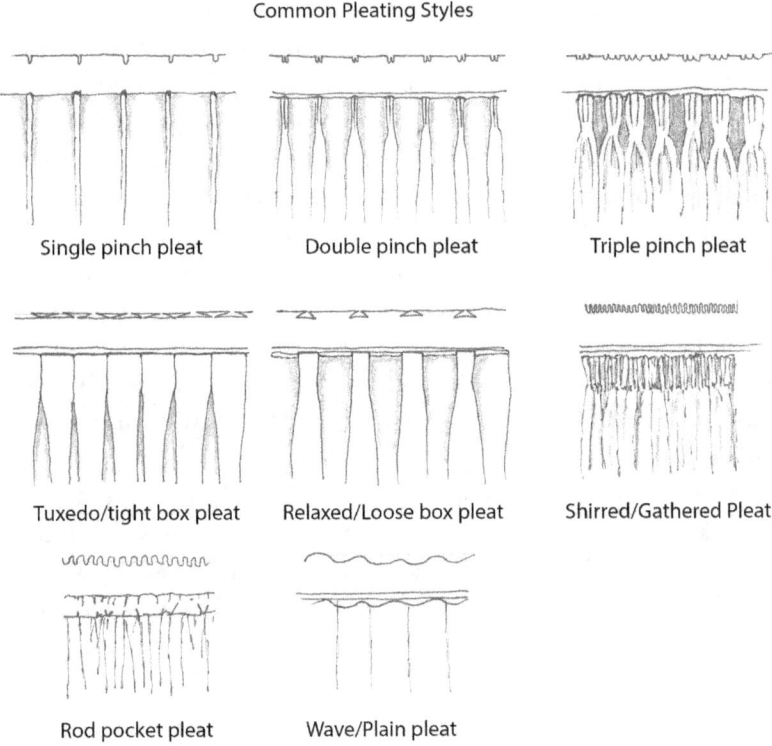

Image 4.2 Illustration showing different drapery styles in front and plan view.
Source: Illustration by the author.

Pleated curtains (the first three examples) generally have metal pleater hooks that you insert into the fabric to create the fullness as illustrated. Commercial pleater tape, which has slots in it for the hooks to insert into, can be purchased and sewn onto the flat curtain panel. Then you install the pleater hooks into the pleater tape. The hooks have a hook on one side that attaches to your curtain rod or a ring and on the other side they have one, two, or three thin metal bars that slide into pockets in the pleater tape to create the gathered look and fullness in the drape.

Box pleated drapes are sewn to give fullness and depth. More specifics about how box pleats are determined and how to create them is detailed in Tip 35 in this chapter.

Shirred or gathered drapes are fairly simple to make. This method of drapery works well with sheers or light weight fabrics. Shirring tape can be purchased and sewn onto a flat panel of fabric. The tape has two strings that run the length of it and you need to be careful to not sew the strings when attaching the tape to the fabric panel. Once the tape is attached you sew across one end of it to capture to strings and keep them in place at one end of the panel. You then begin to pull the strings and gather the fabric. Once you get the panel to the width you want you sew across the shirring tape on the end you have been pulling to lock the length, snip off the extra string and you are done.

Rod pocket pleated drapes are fairly simple to make. You need to determine the rod you will install the drapes on before beginning the process. Once determined you need to measure the circumference of the rod and add ¼ to ½ an inch to the measurement. That number is the size of the pocket you need to sew on the back of the fabric panel. Once the pocket is sewn on you slide the fabric panel on the rod and gather it to your liking.

Wave or plain pleat draperies are probably the simplest drapery to make. Finish the curtain panel edges by hemming and lining as desired. Then either sew on rings, or clip on carriers evenly across the length of your panel. Slide the rings or carriers onto your rod and you are finished.

35 DETERMINING THE SIZE AND NUMBER OF BOX PLEATS IN A DRAPE

Box Pleating typically comes in two styles Tight/Tuxedo pleats or Loose/Relaxed pleats. Tight pleats use more fabric and have a more elegant and richer feel. A 120" wide piece of fabric would net a curtain panel 40" wide when tight pleated. Loose pleats are more spread out and use less fabric. A 120" wide piece of fabric would net a curtain panel 60" wide when loose box pleated. The Formula below can be used to determine the width of each pleat (2X) based on evenly spaced box pleats for both tight and loose box pleats with only one adjustment to the formula. You need to determine the width of your flat curtain panel and the number of pleats you want in the panel when it is complete.

For tight box pleating (As seen in Image 4.3) you will use 6X of fabric for each pleat section. We will use Y to represent the total amount of fabric in a pleat; thus Y=6X. Z represents the total number of pleats you want in your panel of fabric. The formula then looks like this:

Total amount of fabric/number of pleats (Z)= Y

Total amount of fabric/number of pleats (Z)= 6X

Divide both sides by 6 to find X, which is how wide each section of the pleat and spacing can be, a full pleat face is 2X as shown in the image.

Here is an example:

We have a 180" wide fabric panel and want to put 12 pleats in it; the formula would look like this:

180/12 = Y
15=Y
15=6X
2.5=X
5" = 2X

The width of each pleat would be 5". And each return would be 2.5". This curtain would be 60" wide when fully pleated.

Tuxedo/Tight box pleat

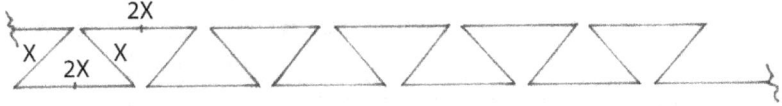

Image 4.3 An illustration showing the layout of tight box pleats in a piece of fabric, showing that for each pleat section you would require 6X of fabric. Source: Illustration by the author.

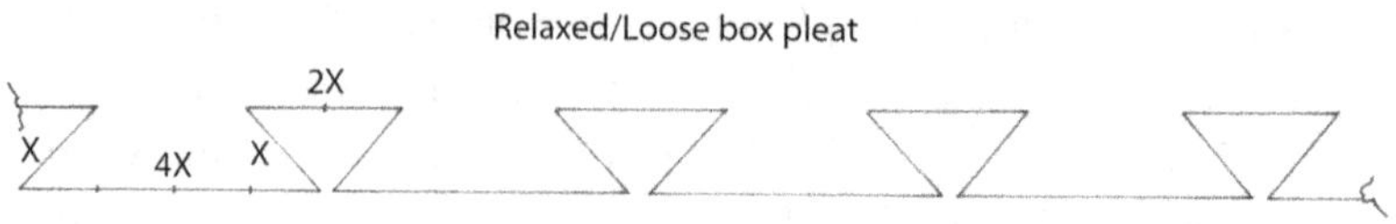

Relaxed/Loose box pleat

Image 4.4 An illustration showing the layout of loose box pleats in a piece of fabric, showing that for each pleat section you would require 8X of fabric.
Source: Illustration by the author.

For loose box pleating (As seen in Image 4.4) you will use 8X of fabric for each pleat section. We will use Y to represent the total amount of fabric in a pleat; thus Y=8X. Z represents the total number of pleats you want in your panel of fabric. The formula then looks like this:

Total amount of fabric/number of pleats (Z) = Y

Total amount of fabric/number of pleats (Z) = 8X

Divide both sides by 8 to find X, which is how wide each section of the pleat and spacing can be, a full pleat face is 2X as shown in the image.

Here is an example:

We have a 120" wide fabric panel and want to put 12 pleats in it; the formula would look like this:

120/12 = Y
10=Y
10=8X
1.25=X
2.5" = 2X

The width of each pleat would be 2.5". And each return would be 1.25". This curtain would be 60" wide when fully pleated.

36 QUICK FULLNESS IN FABRIC

Sometimes, you are asked to cover a window or a doorway with fabric during the tech process, and time is of the essence. We were asked to cover a wall with a "gathered" curtain that was upstage of some doors in a production of Hamlet. This request came during tech, and we were told both the designer and director would love to see it complete after the dinner break. A quick way to add fullness to fabric is to follow these steps. (See Image 4.5 for a visual reference of the steps outlined here.)

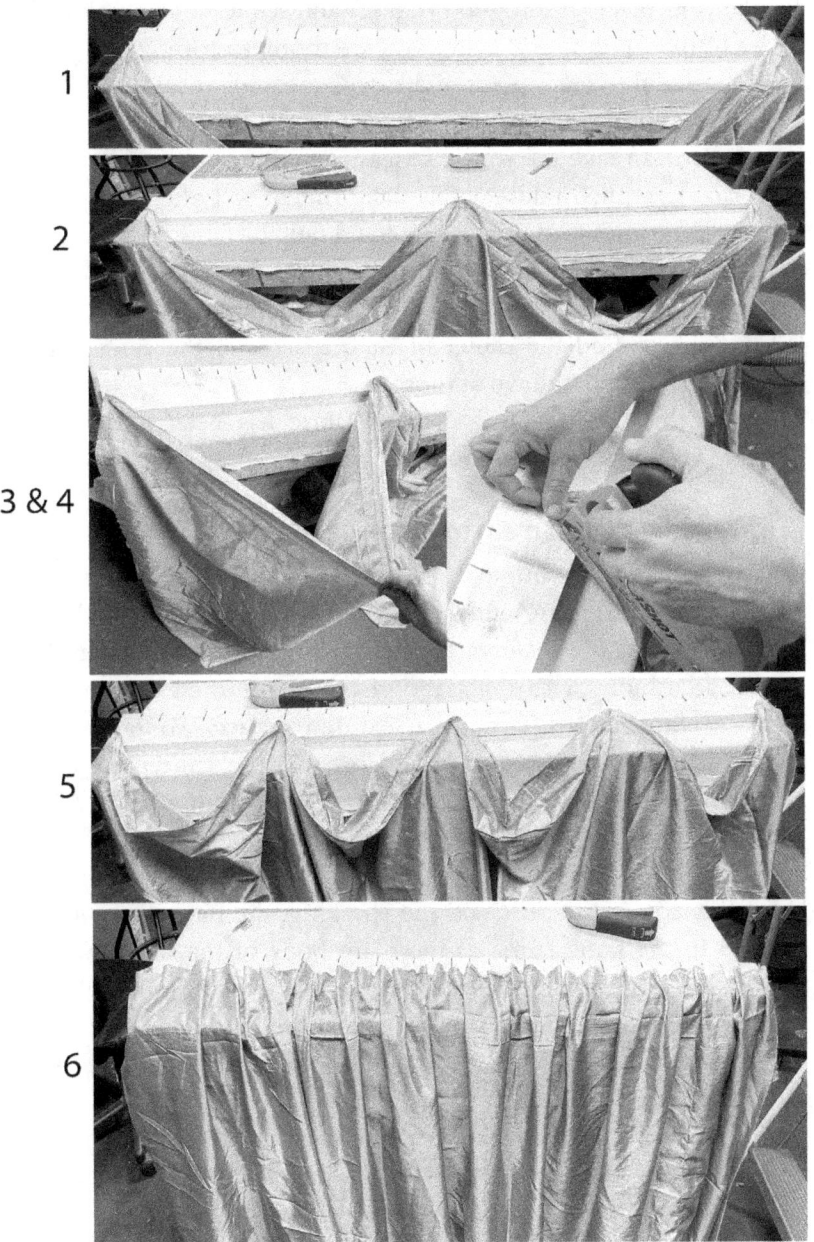

Image 4.5 A series of photos showing the quick fullness method of drapery.
Source: Photos by the author.

1. Take your piece of soft good (fabric) and staple/attach each end to the furthest points of the area you are trying to cover.
2. Then, find the center point of the structure and the fabric and staple that point of the fabric to the center point of the structure.
3. & 4. You can take the time to measure both the structure and the fabric to get the middle point each time, or as I often do, you can eyeball the middle of the structure and pull the fabric away from the structure using one hand until the two sides seem equal and then take that point and staple it to the point you have eyeballed.
5. Continue to find the center of each space and the center of the fabric and staple it down at those spots.
6. Repeat this process until all your fabric has been gathered and stapled to the structure.

37   FABRIC-COVERED BUTTONS FOR UPHOLSTERY

If you do a decent amount of upholstery, you will come across button-tufted furniture, which was particularly popular in the Victorian Era and has a resurgence occasionally. Button tufted furniture has deep cushions where the fabric is pleated into crevices and held in place with buttons, creating a textured surface. We tend to do a lot of furniture upholstery over and over on the same piece of furniture, so we invested in some button-making components. All our button-making dies fit in one of our grommet machines (see Chapter Seven, Tip 72). More specific information about the process of making buttons is covered there. Generally speaking, the buttons want to be covered in the same fabric as the main body of the furniture, so if you have a large piece of furniture you are working on, make sure you get enough additional fabric to make the buttons as well. If you only occasionally need to create buttons many craft stores sell small button-making kits that allow you to make a few buttons for a specific project that are inexpensive and easy to use (Image 4.6).

We did a production of *Antony and Cleopatra* for which our designer wanted us to build an Egyptian chaise. He bought the fabric he wanted for the cushion and mailed it to us. We made the unit to his design and included some fabric-covered buttons to tuft the cushion, as the research image he sent showed. When he arrived at the shop for a check-in, he was surprised to see that we had buttons covered in the same fabric as the fabric he had bought for the piece and asked how

Image 4.6 A photo of a quick button kit from a craft store.
Source: Photo by the author.

we had found matching buttons. I told him we made them. His eyes got huge, and he looked at me incredulously and said: "You can make buttons?" He had been in the industry for years and did not know that was a thing. We still joke about that in our shop.

The backs of the buttons come in several different types, and depending on their use, you will need to determine which you will use (sometimes using more than one on a project). There are nail-in, tie-in, snap, and prong. For a production of *The Matchmaker* (the play version of *Hello Dolly*), our designer wanted the restaurant doors to be button-tufted in red vinyl. We worked with the scenery department to ensure the doors had framing where our buttons would be and used nail-in buttons. Using a rubber-headed mallet or covering the buttons with a scrap piece of fabric is essential to avoid discoloring or marring them when pounding them in. We also have a lovely Victorian button-tufted sofa that we have reupholstered numerous times. Most of the buttons on the back are tied on, but right in the middle of the frame is a structural wood support, so we have to make three buttons that are nail-in, and when we get to that part of the upholstery process we pound those buttons into the wood framing (Image 4.7).

38 PATTERN MATCHING ACROSS FURNITURE PIECES

In a recent production of *Clue*, we had seven matching dining chairs that we were reupholstering into a purple and black brocade. The seat and back shapes were very ornate, and we wanted the patterns to match across the chairs, so we decided to make a template for cutting out the fabric panels. We bought cheap poster frames from a

Image 4.7 A photo showing a settee with deep button tufting across the back, sides, and seat.

Source: Photo by the author.

large box store and removed the thin plastic that covered the poster. We then tacked the fabric to the first chair with a few staples and ensured we were happy with the placement of the pattern. Once we got it correct, we used the transparent plastic sheet and marked on it where the pattern lined up and where the fabric needed to be cut so that the pattern would be consistent across the chairs. We then trimmed the plastic to the correct size, used it to lay out and trace the remaining six chair backs, and cut them out. While this does create exact replications of the fabric, care must still be taken when applying the fabric to the chair so it doesn't get twisted or turned slightly, throwing off the pattern. But if done well, the result is a perfectly matched set of chairs. The same process used for the back of the chairs is repeated for the seats (Image 4.8).

39 FABRIC WEIGHTS AND STRETCHINESS AND WHY IT MATTERS

Having the right fabric for upholstery is essential. You don't want stretchy fabric; it can distort the pattern as you upholster, it can pull

Image 4.8 A photo showing pattern matching on the back and seat upholstery of two chairs (of a set of eight) used for a production of Clue at the Utah Shakespeare Festival.

Source: Photo by the author.

funny or thin out the fabric, allowing for easier punctures or tears, and it will not lie right on the furniture, causing headaches down the road. Work with the designer to ensure the fabric is heavy enough for the project to withstand the abuse and wear and tear the furniture will receive from the performers. Know that, unlike the furniture in your home, it will be stepped on and subject to multiple abuses that regular upholstery would not be. If a stretchy fabric is the perfect fabric, you can iron on interfacing to make it hold its shape (not stretch) and then upholster with it, but depending on how much upholstery you are doing, this can add a lot of time and cost to the project.

We did this for a production of *Richard the Second*. We found some curtains at a local discount store that the designer loved. However, once we started working with the fabric, we realized it was too stretchy, and every time we tried to pull it tight on the chairs, it would warp the design. So, we ironed interfacing onto the back of the fabric and then cut out the pieces. The chairs looked great, and there were no issues with the pattern getting distorted. The material ended up being stiffer and holding up well for an extended period of time.

40 QUICKER UPHOLSTERY

At USF, we tend to reupholster pieces regularly, a chair or sofa appearing in multiple shows over different years, so we have come up with a method of upholstery that, over time saves us labor (though the first time, it is a bit more labor intensive). We upholster each piece in its entirety in muslin the first time we upholster it, we then use the "show fabric and upholster it a second time to get the look the designer is after. The next time we upholster that same piece, we remove the "show fabric" carefully but leave the muslin under layer intact. The show fabric we have pulled off can be used as a pattern to cut the new fabric, and the application of that fabric will be reasonably easy, as we are not fighting with the layers of foam, horsehair, springs, etc. The muslin layer also gives us a smooth surface on which to work, so we don't have bunching of batting or the like that we need to deal with as we upholster. Again, the first time, it takes longer, but when redoing the Victorian button tufted love seat for the sixth time in nine years, that layer of muslin and the show fabric being a pattern for the new fabric is a time saver of epic proportion.

41 PAINT/MARKER STAPLES TO MATCH THE FABRIC COLOR

Depending on the style or period of the chair you are upholstering, you may not be applying gimp or trim to hide your attachment methods. Before you plan to use the staples, you can spray paint or marker the tops of your staples to a color that closely matches the fabric. Then, when you put them in the stapler and staple the fabric on the frame, many of the staples will disappear once they are attached to the fabric/frame. It is much easier than going in with paint or a marker after the fact and trying to cover/mask the staples.

Painting and finishing

Five

Painting and finishing of props can be one of the most rewarding parts of the process. You transform multiple layers of collected material into a unified single object with the addition of paint. Some shops mix their own paints, others use only theatrical paints, and some use store-bought pre-mixed paint colors. There isn't a right or wrong answer here, and at the Utah Shakespeare Festival, we use all these methods to complete the myriad of props we make each year. Knowing how to use the paints and finishes and how to clean them up are some of the important aspects of this area of props. These tips and tricks will help with some of that.

42 ALL THE USES OF THE 5-IN-1 TOOL

The standard 5-in-1 painter's tool features a stainless-steel blade designed to function as a putty knife, a scraper, a gouger, a paint roller cleaner, and a paint can opener, all packed into one multi-faceted device. Sometimes, you have a 6-in-1 or a 7-in-1 tool and don't even know it. If it has a hole in the middle of the blade that functions as a nail puller, and if it has a metal butt that acts as a hammer for setting drywall nails or pounding in staples or nails proud of the surface you are working on (Image 5.1).

43 PAINT CAN MANAGEMENT

One of my biggest pet peeves in the paint area is that people don't clean up the edges of paint cans, and the paint dries in the lip, so when you go to reopen the lid, it can be stuck or messy, and often this leads to you bending the lid or struggling to get the can open, or it cannot seal well and dries out. To solve this issue when we first open a new can of paint, we take a moment and use the pointy part (labeled part #1 in Image 5.1 in the previous tip) of the 5-in-1 tool or a flat-headed screwdriver and a hammer, and punch 3 or 4 holes into the lip of the

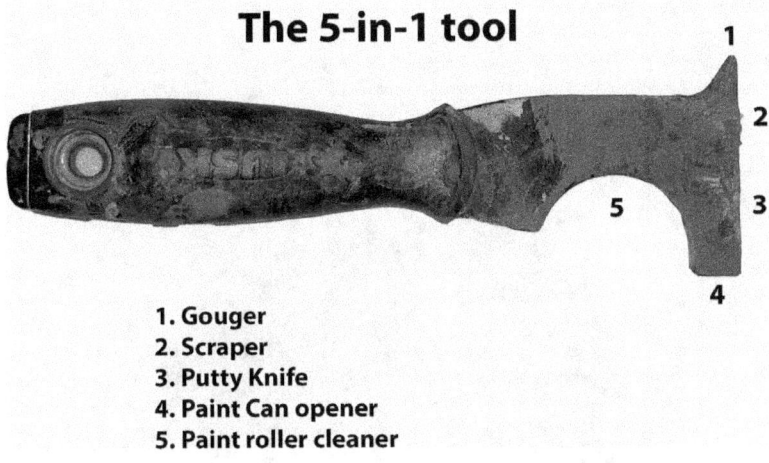

Image 5.1 A photo of a 5-in-1 tool with the parts labeled.
Source: Photo by the author.

paint can so that the holes go through the lip. Then, as we use the can of paint and paint gets into the lip, it drains through the holes back into the can. As we finish painting, we use the brush and run it around the lip of the can to help the paint drip through those holes. Some people think this allows the paint to dry out over time as the can cannot truly seal. I haven't witnessed this, but if you are concerned, you should ensure the little rim is brushed out well so the lid doesn't get stuck. Also, always put a sacrificial rag over the can when pounding the lid closed so that if paint goes flying, it is contained. One final note: when pouring paint out of the can into another container, make sure as you clean up the can that any drips or runs don't cover over important label information like clean-up methods or the paint formula (Image 5.2).

44 THE USE OF GEL STAINS FOR FURNITURE FINISHING

Gel stain is a thicker product than traditional stain and will stick/cling to vertical surfaces. It was introduced commercially in the early 2000s to help DIYers get more consistent staining on projects with vertical surfaces. With traditional stain, the color would often run to the bottom of a vertical surface, so you would end up with a darker lower section and a much lighter top section (and while an Ombre

Image 5.2 A photo showing where to punch holes in a paint can lid for drainage.

Source: Photo by the author.

effect is lovely – probably not on stained furniture as much). Gel stain has a few fantastic properties that work well in the prop world, the biggest of which is that it will dry after being applied over paint. It does take a substantial amount of time to dry when used in this way, but it will dry without having to soak into the pores of the wood like a traditional stain. It allows us to "restain" pieces multiple times over their life in our stock and give them a new look without stripping them down each time, which is caustic and time-consuming.

We will often take a piece of furniture painted a solid color and make that piece look like stained wood again by doing the following steps. Lightly sand the furniture to rough up the surface and remove the seal or gloss it might have on it so the new treatment will stick well to the surface (on occasion, a primer coat might be needed, but often with a light sand, that step is unnecessary). Then, paint the furniture a beige or tan color (depending on the final "stain" color you are going for). Think about the type of wood you are trying to duplicate and choose a base color that is the lightest in that wood in its natural state. Depending on how detailed and realistic you want to be, you can do a scumble or blend of a few colors as the base coat to give it more variation. At this point, I will often do some light dry brushing or graining with a dark brown or black, again picking up on the colors that the wood you are trying to mimic would have in its natural state. For some woods that might mean doing some spatter and drag techniques to create small grain marks like on maple or oak, or in the case of pine using a graining roller to create the undulating look of the grain that species of wood often has. For something like maple or poplar, a good scumbled base coat might be all you need as those woods tend not to have a lot of grain details that would be recognizable. I let the "graining" dry completely and mix up the stain I will use while that is occurring. I take the Gel stain and thin it about 25–30% with the appropriate thinner (the thing the can says cleans up the stain). I mix that well until it is a smooth consistency. Sometimes, I will thin it even more if I want the grain to pop and show through the finished stain, so a thinner stain application would be better with woods with a more pronounced visual grain. (if you have never done this sort of wood staining technique before, take a little time and do some tests with different thick or thin versions of the stain so you achieve the look you are going for.) I then brush the diluted stain onto my prepared "wood." As I brush it on, I work it in a bit so that it allows the graining to show through; it is important (as in real staining) to work in the same direction as the grain so that the brush marks don't show and it looks like it is "flowing" into the pores and grain of the wood (even though our grain is fake we want to give that illusion of reality). I work it in and brush over it until the look and density of stain is to my liking and it visually looks like a piece of stained wood, not a faux painted effect. Once I am happy with the piece's look, I let it dry thoroughly and then apply the sealer coat required to achieve the final look.

What you need to know about gel stain is you need to work it a bit with the wood (painted or raw wood) so that it allows the lower layers to show through. It is so thick that if you brush it on and leave it, it will obliterate any grain or character of the wood; it is like a thick paste and will basically act as paint and completely cover the nature of your wood. This is rarely the effect you want, though it might occasionally be an effective solution, especially with more modern furniture. A cautionary tale about gel stain: I had been using the product for a few years and sharing my love of its versatility with my staff each year. In 2012 We were tasked with building a large calliope for a production of *Scapin* at USF; Walter built this lovely wood structure out of oak veneer-faced plywood and molding. He finished all the sections, and before the final assemble we had another artisan stain all the pieces; I gave them the gel stain and talked them through the process, and then, as often happens, I got called into a meeting and had to leave the shop for about an hour. When I returned, I walked into the shop to check on progress. There were several large pieces of the calliope stained a solid brown color (grain completely gone), as the person applying the stain just painted it on and moved on, not working it in or wiping off excess to allow the grain to show through. Luckily, it was not dry yet, so we grabbed several artisans, the appropriate thinner, and many rags and started soaking them in the thinner and scrubbing the calliope pieces. It took a while, but we were able to remove enough of the stain to restore the grain inherent in the wood and make a beautiful piece.

45 REVIVING DRIED-OUT PAINTBRUSHES

One of my biggest pet peeves is to head to the paint sink at the end of the day and find paintbrushes just sitting in the sink, either sitting in water or, even worse, lying there with dried or drying paint on them. We switched over many years ago to cheaper disposable brushes, but I still want to get more than one use out of these brushes. Sometimes, they have been sitting too long, and just getting them wet and trying to clean them is not going to work. To fix this problem, we soak the brushes in a container of vinegar (or if we don't have any of that we use Murphy's Oil Soap). We leave the brushes soaking in this mixture for several hours to overnight, depending on how badly caked they are. Be sure not to leave the ferrule (the metal part that holds the bristles) in any liquid, as the glue that holds the brush together will soften and the bristles can fall out, making the brush unusable. Also, the ferrule itself, if exposed to too much water, can start to rust and leach that rust into the paint and ruin the brush. Once the brush has soaked, we then go through the normal cleaning process of raking through the bristles with a metal comb to get the large chunks out, rinsing the brush through water, working the bristles with our hands, and making sure that paint that is stuck down inside the bristles get washed out. We finish the cleaning process with a bit of Murphy's oil soap and a final rinse. Once clean, we use our hands to gently coax the bristles to a natural resting place where they are all aligned and headed in the same direction and then hang the brush to dry so we are not deforming the bristles by putting any weight on them.

46 PRE-CLEAN BRUSHES WITH A DROP OF SOAP

Another quick brush-cleaning trick I learned from a painter friend is if you put a small drop of dish soap on a brush and work it into the bristles before you begin painting, it will not really affect the paint but will allow the brush to clean up a bit easier when you are done with it. I find this trick to be particularly effective with things like water-based contact adhesive and white glue, where the material being spread can be a bit thicker and also "sticky" in a way, so by having the soap already in the bristles allows you to get more out of the brush and maybe save it for several uses before having to discard it. I always use a cheap disposable brush when dealing with contact adhesive or glue, as the brush will get destroyed over time, no matter what precautions you take.

47 CHEAPER VERSION OF CRACKLE FINISH

We sometimes use a crackle paint finish to show age; this allows a base color of paint to show through cracks of later layers of paint, exposing one or more previous layers of paint. There are commercial crackle glazes on the market, but we have found that using white glue is a simple way to mimic this effect at a much-reduced cost. We apply a base layer or layers of paint and let them dry. Then we apply a layer of white glue over the surface we want to crackle, and while the glue is still wet we apply the top layer of paint over the glue. As the glue and paint dry, the top layer cracks apart to get oxygen to the white glue for it to set/dry. The longer we wait to apply the top layer of paint, the more minor the cracks in the top coat will be. If we want giant cracking, we apply the top layer right after we get the glue spread. Depending on the shop environment and humidity levels, we sometimes need to work in sections so the glue does not dry before we can apply the top coat. Some testing for this type of effect is always recommended.

48 SILK SCREENING

Silk screening is a stenciling method that involves printing ink through stencils that are supported by a porous fabric mesh stretched across a frame called a screen. The stencil is made by using a photo emulsion spread onto a very fine fabric mesh. When the emulsion is subjected to a high-powered light source, it hardens while the area that is covered by the graphic remains soft and is washed out of the mesh. That area is where the ink passes through the mesh to print onto the substrate. Silk screening is a great way to create a specific printed look on props or costume pieces for a production. Over the years, we have had professional silk screens made for flags, large fabric panels, and other uses. To this day, if I needed a large (bigger than 11×17) screen I would send the artwork out to be made because the creation of the screen is the most crucial part and large screens can be challenging to get right if you are not set-up with all the right equipment. Several years ago, we were introduced to EZ Screen, a silkscreen creation process made for the home crafter that requires little prep and produces outstanding results with little effort. The screens come sealed in a dark protective sleeve with emulsion already on them. You print your artwork onto clear acetate, and using that artwork image, a towel, and the sun, you can, in just a few minutes, expose your emulsion screen to the sun with your artwork on it and then, working in a dark room, wash your screen, removing the unhardened emulsion (producing your artwork on the screen). Then, depending on how you use it, you can mount it to a traditional screen frame or use it freehand.

The prop and costume departments have used it many times for different effects. In a production of *The Tempest*, the costume shop created a robe for Prospero covered with snippets from Leonardo Da Vinci sketchbooks; they created 6–8 small (8 × 8 screen images) and using different colors of ink and rotating the images, were able to cover the robe with sketches and journal entries. In both The Diary of Anne Frank and The Music Man, we needed cardboard boxes with specific logos on them; in Anne Frank, the canning company that Anne's father worked for (Opekta), and for The Music Man, we needed a musical instrument company logo for the boxes that came off the Wells Fargo wagon. We created the logos in Adobe Photoshop, printed them out, and followed the directions on the EZ Screen material. We built traditional silk screen frames to hold the EZ Screen material for ease of use and silk-screened the boxes. With some newer technologies, there is the potential to use a vinyl cutter, laser cutter, or even a CNC to create a stencil, which would give a similar effect, but sometimes making a quick silk screen will give you just the look you are after. Either way, getting to know and understand the basics of silk screening is a great trick to have in your arsenal for those particular projects when you might need them (Image 5.3).

49 THE BASICS OF DISTRESSING FURNITURE

There are so many ways to do this that it is hard to nail down specific tips and tricks, but I want to start by talking about one thing that I think is super important: understanding the distressing of an object. In my early career, I would start sanding down the furniture and or spattering on glaze or washes without thinking about how it should really look. That is terrible! We spend some time thinking about how the piece would be used/handled and how easy parts of it are to clean. We look at samples of aged furniture to understand how things naturally age over time so that the distressing we are doing makes sense and looks correct when viewed onstage. The footrest on a chair is going to get scuffed and marred by people putting their feet on it, and the carvings on a piece of furniture are going to gather dirt and grime first and will be harder to clean, so over time, it will get darker and more gacked up. The front edges of arms on chairs will get lighter and more abused as people use them to push out of chairs, etc. The front edges of chair seats, particularly toward the center, get rubbed first as our legs contact those areas of the chair. I think there are two main types of distressing: adding visual dirt and age and showing physical wear and tear. Each will be discussed in more detail in the two following tips. The biggest thing to remember is that when you step back from

Image 5.3 A photo showing multiple screens we have made for different projects using the EZ screen.
Source: Photo by author.

the piece and place it on stage, the aging and distressing you have done should look believable and real (Image 5.4).

50 THE IMPORTANCE OF HIGHLIGHT AND SHADOW

Very early in my career, I was hired to work at a summer stock at my college. We finished building the three shows for the summer season early, and they asked several of us to stay on and begin work on the fall musical (*West Side Story*), which was going to be a massive production. There was a ton of scenery, and the designer was concerned about achieving all the detail he wanted for the molding on all of the units while maintaining some fiscal responsibility. He knew he could not afford decorative crown molding and fancy baseboards in the scale the show called for with the budget available. So, we created the look of all these moldings using one-by and two-by and stacking them in different ways per the designer's specs. From the audience's point of

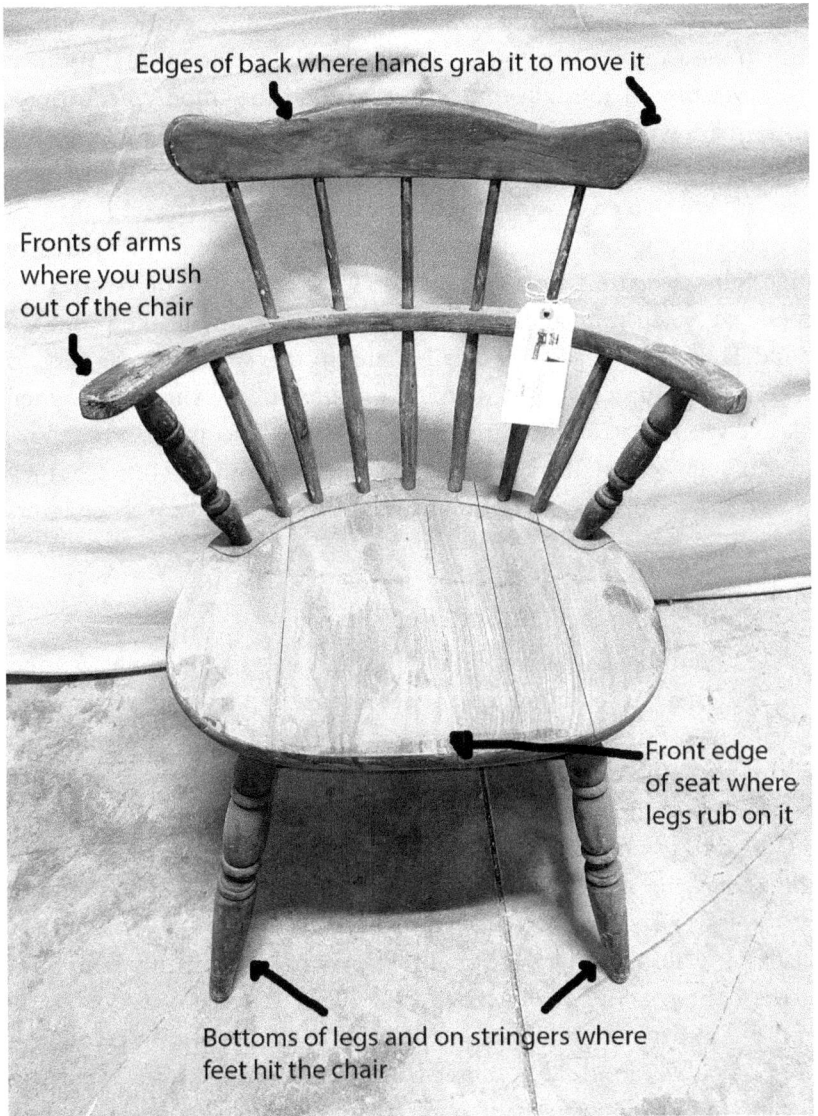

Image 5.4 A photo showing the areas where a chair will show the most wear.

Source: Photo by the author.

view, in our large auditorium, they could not see how the molding was created. Still, they saw various lines of highlight and shadow as the lighting hit the multiple levels of wood we had assembled to mimic the expensive moldings we couldn't afford. They saw (or their eyes tricked them into thinking they saw) substantial expensive moldings due to the nature of shadow as the theatrical lighting hit the wood.

It was one of the first times I understood the importance of creating shadow lines. They help to define space visually for our brains. A producer I worked with years ago once said, "We perceive coolness because we perceive warmth." he was talking about visual light in a theatrical setting. In the same way, I would extrapolate that we perceive highlights because we perceive shadows. It is one of the reasons we spend so much time adding layers of detail to many of the props we build. Those added layers of detail do not read as specifically as they do when we are up close and working on them in the shop. Still, when blasted with theatrical lighting, they create depth, texture, and shadow, which helps to give the surface of the objects life and vitality that they would not have if we had not taken the time to build up those layers to fool the audience's eye.

51 ADDING VISUAL DIRT AND AGE

I have found the easiest way to add dirt and age is by using glazes and washes. There is a difference between glazes and washes, and both have their uses in aging/distressing a prop. A wash is a paint thinned with water (the main part (of paint) being an opaque medium), and a glaze is a transparent or semi-transparent medium to which color is added. So, when dry, a paint wash will tend to obscure more of the underlying layer, while a glaze will tend to tint it and allow more of the lower layer to be seen. We use a lot of glazes and washes for distressing things. There are multiple pre-made glazes for people to distress their kitchen cabinets and the like that we use in our work. You can also add colorant to a clear glaze to create custom colors. We are particularly fond of the water-based Asphaltum glaze and an aging compound called Java Glaze, which was designed to make kitchen cabinets look worn. Being glazes, they have a transparent base.

Following the idea about how furniture ages discussed above, we apply the glaze (often with a sponge or a rag) to the nooks and crannies of a piece, making sure it settles into the deepest parts of the carvings or that it puddles up into joints. We use different painting mediums to represent dirt and the buildup of gak and age, so we work it into crevices and deep into carved sections. One way to do this is to apply the glaze liberally to the entire area and then use a rag or towel to wipe off the upper layers so the "dirt" settles into the lower areas of the piece making them seem dirtier, as they would not get cleaned as easily. We then wipe away as needed to provide levels of dirt and grim. For fabric, we will spray these same glazes onto them or spatter the fabric piece with diluted bleach (always do this outside in a safe and contained manner) to allow the color to fade on the fabric. Be aware that you might need to wash the fabric to stop the bleach from eating the material away; also, know the longer the bleach is on the fabric, the more distressed the fabric will look. Quick sprays of spray paint are another way we quickly add age and dirt to objects.

52 SHOWING PHYSICAL WEAR AND TEAR

Sometimes, just adding painted aging is not enough and we need to rough up the surface. Actual physical distressing can be particularly important in smaller spaces or if the audience will be close to the objects. This is particularly true for us in our black box theater, where often the audience walks across the stage to get to their seats so they are right next to the props. Before we attack the furniture, we think about how the object is used, how it is referred to in the play, what abuse or use it has seen over its life, how long the piece has been around, and how much abuse it gets daily from what would be years of use. Once we have these ideas in mind, we attack the object with the requisite tools to give it that used and abused look appropriate for the show.

We tend to use drywall rasps, heavy grit sandpaper, chain, and sometimes sandblasting. Also, at times, we will use an Adze (also known as a draw knife) or a wood grinding disc in a handheld grinder to remove lots of material from the edges of the wood to show lots of use and wear. We sand edges to remove finish and stain, we sandblast the furniture to show massive age or weathering, and sometimes we will take a length of chain to the piece to beat divots into the surfaces. Be careful with how hard you hit an item; while doing this once I had a door to a nightstand fly off because I was hitting the furniture too hard with the chain. We will also, at times, carve gouges into surfaces using chisels, knives, etc. Something to remember when doing physical distressing is that you probably will only be able to return the piece to the pre-distressed version with considerable work, so make sure the distressing is a good choice for your stock.

For fabric distressing, we snip with scissors and then tear rips into the fabric; we use drywall rasps to rough up the surface and pull up threads, creating snags. For one history play, the designer wanted the battle banners to be particularly distressed, so we attached them to the bumper of our shop van and dragged them around our gravel parking lot for a bit. Many of the same techniques and tools we use on wood furniture can be used when distressing upholstered furniture. We often start with sanding the fabric and then use drywall rasps to snag and pull up strings (paying attention to the same wear patterns you would see on wood furniture). Sometimes we even use paint or a wash to paint in butt prints, particularly in the fabric that has a bit of nap; the paint will help to lay that nap down/flatten it so it reads as worn without us physically wearing that area away. This is a good thing to keep in mind; when doing physical distressing, you don't want to weaken the wood or fabric to the point where it will break or rip due to the distressing you have done. Be aware of how much you are abrading things when doing this; you can use products like Fray-check or fusible interfacing to reinforce the fabric after distressing it so it doesn't continue to degrade once you have gotten it to the desired level of aging.

Crafts and effects

Six

The number of things that fall under "crafts" and "effects" in props is ridiculously huge. There are so many craft skills that after over 30 years in the business, I still learn new things every season. Entire books could be written about this one aspect of the job. I am only going to hit on the highlights and a few specific things that have really saved me over the years I have been at the Utah Shakespeare Festival. Learn any and every craft skill you can; they will all be invaluable during your career.

53 COLORED HOT GLUE FOR SEALING WAX

We produce a lot of documents for shows, particularly for our Shakespeare productions, many with "royal" or official seals. These can be either to seal the document or to stamp the document next to the signature to make it look official. Traditionally, this was done with sealing wax, which requires the use of fire and can be messy and hard to work with if you are not familiar with the process. It can be especially time-consuming if making multiple copies for a long production run. We found a company (there are now several out there) that makes colored hot glue to mimic the look of sealing wax. It is marketed to people doing wedding invitations and the like.

We use this product to make faux wax seals for our documents. The process is relatively easy and makes a very convincing-looking seal. Generally, we do not make the seals directly on the documents but create them on a sheet of waxed paper. This allows us to control size and shape a little better and allows for quality control. If we make a bad one, it hasn't destroyed a paper prop. Before we begin, we determine the size and color we want for the seal and choose the image we want inset into the "wax." We have found and purchased nearly two dozen wax stamps over the last decade, everything from crosses to crowns. We also use metal coins as a stamp sometimes. To help with size control, we sometimes print out a sheet with circle images on it, the size we want the seals to be, and slide it under the waxed paper so we have a target.

To make the seals, we put the appropriate color of hot glue into a glue gun (we have one dedicated to this purpose). We run out the old color and make generic seals using the previous color for future use. Once the color we need comes through the gun, we begin making the seals. We apply the hot glue in a circle, filling in the entire area but slightly smaller than our finished size as the "wax" will smoosh out slightly when we stamp it. We then push the stamp into the glue, let it set for a few seconds, and then pull it away. We have found that keeping the stamp cool is critical for a clean image, so we will often dip it in cold water or allow enough time to let it cool between uses. Once the wax seals are cooled, we either peel them off the wax paper or trim the wax paper to the edges so it is not noticeable.

Then, depending on how we use the letter, we will determine the best attachment method for the seal. If the letter is never opened onstage, we will attach the seal with some hot glue. If the letter is opened on stage, we will use hot glue on one side of the letter fold and then use a glue dot on the other side to hold it closed but allow it to be easily opened on stage. The glue dots typically last for a few performances before they need to be replaced. We also often color coordinate seals in a show so we know from whom each letter comes (Image 6.1).

54 FUGITIVE GLUE

Fugitive Glue (credit card adhesive), or as we affectionately refer to it, Gorilla snot, is like hot glue but remains more flexible. It is a low-tack hot melt adhesive that forms a temporary bond. It was designed for use in direct mail campaigns to adhere samples and credit cards to larger mail pieces. The bond formed is strong enough to keep the item in place but weak enough that the item can be removed with little or no damage. It is designed to leave no residue on either surface when they have been separated. We have found that to be relatively accurate. However, it reacts poorly with some fake foods (creating a nasty oily residue) and does not work on all fabrics, occasionally leaving some staining. Compared to the damage we were incurring with hot glue;

Image 6.1 A photo showing a sample collection of seals made with the hot glue sealing wax.
Source: Photo by the author.

Fugitive Glue is way easier to deal with. It is fantastic for dressing sets, attaching objects to shelves, carts, baskets, tables, you name it. It remains flexible and sticky for a long time, so it also adheres better than hot glue on many surfaces.

The kind we use comes in metal tubes that slide into a dispensing gun. There is a base heater unit that needs to plug into an electrical socket with a round receptacle that the glue tube slides into with the handle attached. The heating coil heats the glue to a more liquid state so it can flow out of the tube. You then remove the glue gun from the coil and use the applicator (like a hot glue gun) to apply the "snot" to the objects and adhere them. The glue will start to cool down if left outside the heating unit for a long time, so keep that in mind when working with it. You are basically cordless when using the glue, but if you keep it outside the heating unit for too long, you might need to wait several minutes after you put the gun back in the base units for the glue to get back to a flow state where it can be used again.

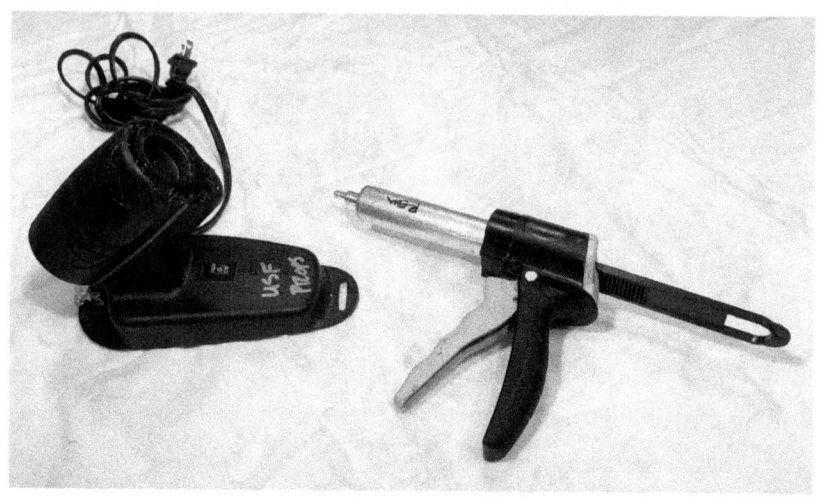

Image 6.2 A photo showing a fugitive glue heating element and applicator gun.
Source: Photo by the author.

There is also a cold option that comes in rolls like tape but is just a sticky snot-like substance that you can use similarly. I prefer the glue option that heats up as it is easier to apply and tends to do a better job of temporarily bonding the two items together (Image 6.2).

55 SETTING VINYL WITH LIQUID

We are often asked to adhere adhesive craft vinyl to surfaces to create signs or use as a resist. Many vinyls are very sticky, and if they get stuck down in the wrong spot, it can be a pain to nearly impossible to rearrange or shift. We spray the substrate to which we are applying the vinyl with a liquid solution, then lay the vinyl down. This wet technique allows us to adjust the vinyl and get it situated just right before we squeegee it and stick it down permanently. The liquid solution we have found works best is a mix of about 80% water, 20% rubbing alcohol, and four drops of dish soap. We spray the area well, lay the vinyl on the wet surface, shift it around to get it where we want it, and then apply a little pressure to adhere it lightly. We then work from the center out using our brayer or squeegee and slowly push the liquid out from under the vinyl. Once it is adhered to the substrate and most of the liquid has been squeezed out, we let the backing dry and then carefully peel it off, leaving the vinyl decal stuck down exactly where we need it.

56 REMOVING AIR BUBBLES

Even with the liquid setting method mentioned above, an air bubble will occasionally get stuck under or in the vinyl. We take a sharp pin (often a sewing pin) and poke a hole in the vinyl as close to the middle of the air bubble as possible. Then, we use the application squeegee or brayer and work the air out from under the vinyl using the tiny hole(s) we created. If the bubble is large, you might need to cut a slit with a razor blade to allow the air to escape. On occasion, with a really stubborn bubble the addition of some heat (from a hair dryer) might help to allow the vinyl to stretch and release the air trapped under it. Just be careful not to heat up the vinyl to the point where it warps or stretches out of shape.

57 USE BALL CHAIN WHEN WIRING

When rewiring a light fixture, be it a sconce or a chandelier, it can be hard to get the wires through the twists and turns of the arm(s). We fish a length of small ball chain through the arm so it sticks out both ends; we then use some craft wire and electrical tape to adhere and attach the electrical wire to the ball chain. We do this by taking a little bit of floral wire and wrapping it tightly around the ball chain and the electrical wire two or three times, pulling it tight so the wire sits between the balls on the ball chain. We then tape over that connection with a wrap or two to help hold it all together. You don't want to make your connection to fat as it needs to slide through the arm smoothly. We add a bit of dish soap or shampoo to the wire's beginning and then use the ball chain to pull the wire through the arm. It is essential to feed the wire into the arm and not to pull too hard on the ball chain, or it might separate from the wire. It is also helpful to use gravity to your advantage by turning or twisting the arm so the chain or wire falls through the arm in the same direction as gravity; this is useful when putting the ball chain in initially and feeding the wire through. Consistent pressure and smooth movements will help slide the wire through the curves of the arm and allow it to pop out the other end. Thereby getting the wire through the piece and allowing you to electrify the prop with new wire (Image 6.3).

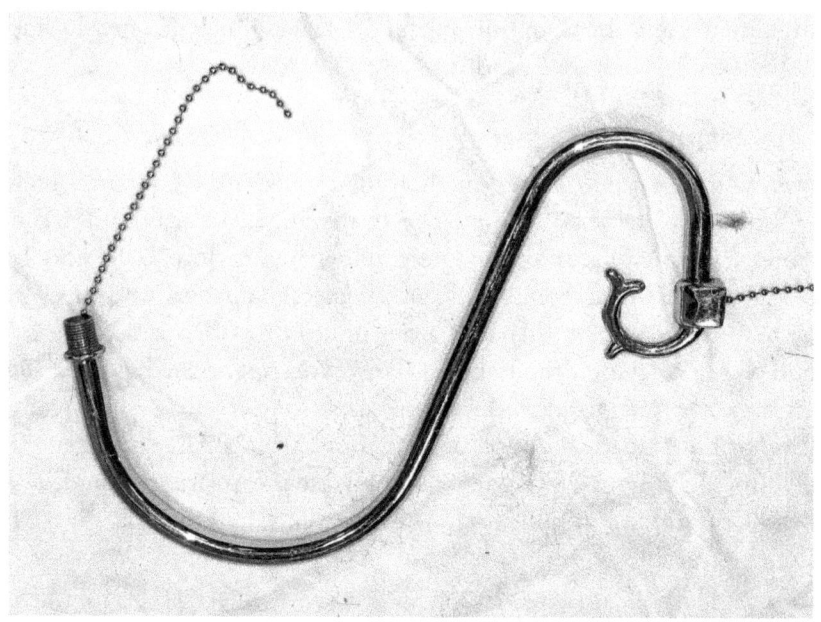

Image 6.3 A photo showing ball chain running through a sconce arm to allow the pulling of wire through the interior channel.
Source: Photo by the author.

58 EVA FOAM

Recently, we have been asked to make pickaxes, sledgehammers, and railroad mauls for two different musicals. Performers in musical numbers would use these items, and both directors wanted the actors to be able to hit the floor with the tools on percussive moments in the music. This set off alarm bells as these tools, while not sharp, are heavy; some are pointy and could wreak much damage to performers and the floor if not handled carefully. After some research and tests, we determined to make them out of Ethylene-Vinyl Acetate, or EVA foam.

EVA foam is a closed-cell foam. It is often used in floor and exercise mats, sports equipment, crafts, kickboards, life jackets, and flip-flops. EVA foam can be shaped with heat, glued to itself or other materials, machined, and painted. EVA foam comes in various thicknesses, shapes, and density. It is a very versatile foam product that is lightweight and very solid in its visual makeup. It cuts and machines very cleanly and maintains an edge well. It is a staple of the cosplay world and is used extensively for armor and weapons. It is now available at many online sources, as well as in major craft stores and big box chains. It is often referred to as cosplay foam.

One of the most important things to remember when working with this foam is to use sharp utensils; if the knife (knives) you use are not sharp, you will tear the foam rather than cut it, leaving rough edges and tear marks that will take a long time to clean up. There are so many ways to work with this product and clever tools and tricks that entire books have been written about it. I won't try to explain them all here. I recommend you look on YouTube or Pinterest for EVA tricks and you will find more information than you can possibly need.

59 AGING/DISTRESSING PAPER

There are as many ways of aging and distressing paper as there are prop people. A few that we use at the Utah Shakespeare Festival regularly are:

a. Edge wear/distressing. A common way to give paper more age is to deckle the edge of the paper. Deckling is the ripping or cutting of the paper edge to provide it with a more rustic homemade (non-manufactured) look. Depending on the weight of the paper, there are a few ways to achieve the effect. On heavier papers, we tend to fold the paper back and forth on a crease line we create, and for really heavy papers, we might even wet that folded edge and then rip the paper off to pull the straight edge off and leave a softer more fibrous edge in its place. This will also obviously change the paper size slightly, making it look more period because it will not be a standard (modern) size that the audience will instantly recognize. If the paper is thinner (regular weight copy paper, for example), then we will often take a ruler and lie it on top of the paper inset a little bit (1/2" to ¾") and then grab the thin strip of paper that is exposed on the side of the ruler and pull up the edge use the ruler as a guide to rip that thin edge off the paper. Without the water and multiple back-and-forth folds, this style creates a rougher, more homemade edge to the paper. It is important to consider how the edges of the paper are being finished for any given show so that when the text is laid out, it will allow for that edge ripping or other edge finish without losing any of the words on the document. Once we have distressed/aged the edge of the paper, we can use one of the following methods to give the surface of the paper some needed aging and distressing, depending on the final desired result.

b. Amber shellac – This heavy-duty treatment creates a reasonably robust aging. For this to work well, the document needs to be copied on a copier printed on a laser printer so that the ink is "heat set"; otherwise, the ink can run and smear when the shellac is brushed over it. This will happen with nearly any document printed on an inkjet printer. The process involves making a few more copies of the document than you think you will need for the length of your run. We typically use beige paper with a little visual breakup on the surface for making the copies. We cover the work surface with waxed paper and lay out the copies of the document(s). We thin down the amber shellac about 50/50 with denatured alcohol and stir it well. We then take a brush and distribute the shellac over the surface of the documents; we don't want even or straight brush strokes, so we tend to use the scumble technique, but with only the single color of shellac. Once the document is covered with the shellac and we have worked it enough not to see brushstrokes, we let it dry. If we want the document to have more surface texture or to show more age, we will take some additional shellac and spatter it over the document. Once the paper has completely dried, we peel it off the waxed paper, flip it over, and give the back the same treatment (one of my pet peeves is seeing a really good paper prop that is not double-sided. We always try to treat all the surfaces so that no matter what the audience sees it reads as authentic.). After the back has had substantial time to dry, we stack the document(s) for use in the show. We have found that if left for a long time, they tend to stick together, especially in the presence of moisture (humidity) or heat. Hence, we tend to stack them with waxed paper between each copy to be more easily separated when needed.

c. Tea dipping or spraying paper with tea or coffee. This is just what it sounds like. We often use tea dyeing to change the color of linens and fabric and give them some age, to take off the newness of color; the same idea works for paper as well, and depending on how old we want the paper to be will help to determine the amount of coffee (darker) or tea (lighter) we will use the age the papers being distressed. We want to protect our worksurface by covering it with moisture-absorbing materials. We want to keep the water (tea or coffee) from unintentionally seeping onto or aging the surface. Once the area is covered, we lay out our document(s). We brew our tea or coffee as we would for drinking; the hot water activates the crystals in the drink and helps it to set in the paper. Once we have mixed up our liquid, we can dunk/soak our document(s) in the liquid and then lay them out to dry on the prepared surface, or we can put the tea or coffee in a spray bottle and mist the documents with the spray function (not Stream!). We are always aware that the liquid may be hot, so we wear gloves or hand protection not to burn ourselves when handling these hot liquids. Once dry, if we sprayed them, we must flip them over and spray the other side to complete the aged look on the document(s). Something else we consider when doing this method (particularly the dunking method) is that the paper will wrinkle some, which often adds to the texture and aged look of the document(s) and is quite effective. One way to reduce that wrinkling is to weigh the papers down while they dry, which requires us to lay down a towel-like object (something that will absorb some of the moisture well) on top of the letters and then to evenly distribute weight on top of that towel while the document(s) dry out.

d. Glossy Wood Tone spray paint. Design Master makes a full line of translucent spray paints (typically used for tinting live flowers), which are great for aging and distressing not only paper but nearly any item. The best color for prop work is Glossy Wood Tone. They also have a translucent black and a whitewash, which are great, as well as numerous additional colors. It was hard to find most of these for a while, but they are now back in production and if you are unfamiliar with them, you should buy a couple of cans and experiment to learn how they can be useful to you. Just note that they are not cheap, so once you figure out their uses, make sure the staff in the shop know they are not just for any old project. Use them when appropriate.

60 SOFTENING/WEARING DOWN PAPER

Used paper has a softness to it from being handled; money is an excellent example of this. If we have a paper prop that needs to feel used and handled, we will often put that prop with a reasonably damp (not dripping wet) towel in the dryer. We then run the dryer through a typical drying cycle (often on low heat so the paper doesn't get too hot). The most common item we do this with is money, so inevitably, an artisan walks in while I am doing this and makes some joke about laundering money.

61 THE PRINTING OF FAUX CURRENCY FOR THEATRICAL USE

Since I am telling you that we print fake money, I should point out that one crucial thing to know about producing prop money, particularly US money (and I am sure other countries have similar rules), is that you need to modify the money in very specific ways to make sure you are within the law. The most recent official US statute for fake currency has the following stipulations, which must ALL be met for the fake currency not to be considered counterfeit.

The resolution should be at most 72 dpi for digital copies and the illustration must be of a size less than three-fourths or more than one and one-half, in linear dimension, of each part of the item illustrated; the illustration is one-sided; and all negatives, plates, positives, digitized storage medium, graphic files, magnetic medium, optical storage devices, and any other thing used in the making of the illustration that contains an image of the illustration or any part thereof are destroyed and deleted or erased after their final use. 18 U.S.C. 504(1)

62 SLIP-CASTING GREENWARE FOR BREAKAWAYS

Slip casting is a technique used to create intricately shaped pottery/ceramics that are difficult or impossible to make using traditional methods such as throwing or hand-building. The process involves using a slip-cast mold, a porous mold made of plaster, or another similar material. The mold absorbs the moisture from the slip, causing it to solidify and take on the shape of the mold. The process of slip casting involves pouring a liquid clay mixture, called slip, into the mold, allowing the slip to solidify to a desired thickness, pouring out the remaining liquid slip to be reused, allowing the remaining slip to harden in the mold for a period of time, and then removing the mold to reveal the desired shape. The cast item until it is fired in a kiln is referred to as greenware.

We tend to make slip-cast dishes, vases, etc., when asked for a breakaway for a show. Generally, it is a relatively cheap and fast way to produce these objects and is not a complicated process to learn or master. There is potential for good options to 3-D print breakables, and I will discuss that a little bit in the 3-D printing section of the technology chapter. (Chapter Seven, Tip 76) Some examples of breakaways we have made include the vase in *Mary Poppins* that gets dropped and shatters, revealing the father's stars, the vase in *Murder for Two* that gets shot at and explodes from on top of the piano, and the vase that gets thrown and shatters in *The Play That Goes Wrong*.

Hundreds of molds exist from different ceramic companies, and with a bit of practice, you can also make your own molds. The molds are made of plaster, which absorbs and then slowly dissipates moisture. Most plaster molds for slip casting are multi-part, generally two parts, but they can be more than that. The ceramic slip can be purchased from a clay or ceramic supplier; it comes in various types and finishes that fire in a kiln with different results. We generally do not fire our molded items, so I usually only worry a little about the particulars of the slip we order. I only ensure it is for ceramics (not porcelain or china).

Once the slip and mold(s) are all acquired, the process of making the greenware can begin. First, we secure the mold with straps, rubber bands, or another device to keep the parts of the mold in good contact with each other. We want to ensure the mold stays together well, but we don't need to apply a ton of pressure or risk possibly cracking the plaster. Once it is secure, we place it on a metal baking sheet so that if it overflows, we do not get liquid slip on our work surface. We then fill the mold with the liquid slip to the top. Depending on the mold size, sometimes we need to add a bit more as the forming process takes place because as the moisture is drawn out of the slip, the "liquid" slip level will fall within the mold. Some experimentation is required at this point based on the location, humidity, etc. We find that leaving the slip in the mold for anywhere from 2 to 10 minutes gives us a suitable wall thickness; this is where the experimentation is crucial. Shop conditions, humidity, temperature, and others vary widely, so knowing how long the slip takes to set up and give a suitable wall thickness is essential to establish. The wall thickness needs to be enough to support the object once it is dry but not so thick that it does not consistently break when it is supposed to. I have found that a wall thickness of 3/16ths – ¼" works well; on occasion, we will go to 3/8" thick for larger pieces, but much more than that generally makes the piece too thick to break well.

For the first couple of casts, we experiment a bit; we pour in the slip, set a timer for a set period, then pour the remaining liquid slip back into the original container and allow the ceramic cast to dry in the mold for 30–60 minutes and then free it to check for thickness. Once we have established the time we need to leave the slip in the mold to get the desired thickness, we are ready to begin mass-producing our greenware. (Even after we have figured out the timing for a particular mold and slip combination, we will sometimes find that a significant change in humidity or temperature in the workspace causes the cast to be too thin or too thick, so we adjust as needed during the casting process). We set up a station, prepare the mold, pour in the slip, let it set for the predetermined amount of time, and then pour out the liquid slip (back into a storage container). Then, we let the mold sit with the casting inside for an additional period (again, this will vary widely based on location, humidity, etc.). During our summers, it might only take 15–20 minutes, but in the winter, when we have much more humidity, we have sometimes found we might need to leave the greenware in the mold for up to 24 hours before it is strong enough to remove. Once we can see that the casting is pulling away from the plaster mold, it is okay to remove it. We open the mold, remove the slip-cast object, and place it on a smooth surface to air dry for a day or two, depending on the conditions in the shop. Generally, we also want the mold to sit for a bit (a few hours) to dissipate the moisture from the plaster before doing another casting.

Then we have to make a choice: to fire or to air-dry further. Firing greenware in a kiln makes it stronger (turning it more into a ceramic or porcelain object); however, it tends to make it brittle and has sharp edges when it breaks. So, we often pour our vases a wee bit thicker (leave them in the mold a few more minutes) and then let them air dry for an extended period, as long as two weeks, to really allow all the moisture to release from the object and for it to strengthen. It will still be slightly delicate, but if handled correctly, it can be used in the production until it is time to break. When unfired greenware is broken, it tends to powder up a bit and be soft on the edges, allowing for a safer process for the performers in the breaking. Once our object(s) are air-dried, we paint and finish them as required for the design (Image 6.4).

63 GEL WAX IN BOTTLES AND GLASSES FOR "LIQUID"

We often need liquid in bottles but don't want to deal with the liquid molding over a long run, or the bottles are just sitting on a bar cart or in a cabinet and never get moved. Also, the director sometimes asks

Image 6.4 Photos showing a plaster mold open (top), the mold ready for pouring (bottom left) and a vase that came out of the mold (bottom right).
Source: Photos by the author.

for a clear drinking vessel and wants to see the liquid in the glass, but the actors will never consume the drink. We have taken to coloring gel wax to the correct color corresponding to whatever liquid is used and filling the bottles and or glasses with the gel wax. It is a transparent base, and the colorant additives are also on the transparent side, so it looks like liquid. We have found that there are times when filling the bottle or drinking vessel can be helpful as it gives a very realistic look (black box space). Still, other times, we pour a small amount of the colored gel wax into the object, tilt it, and rotate the vessel so the wax coats the outside to a specified level. We keep turning the vessel for a bit so that the wax continues moving around as it cools and hardens to get a consistent thickness in the vessel. This is helpful when we don't want the vessel to get top-heavy (champagne flutes are the biggest culprit). It also allows the bottles and drinking vessels to be lighter than if they were full, making them more manageable for the actors to handle and work with, and a bonus is that it saves a lot of gel wax. If, at a future date, we want to change the color of the liquid, we can put the glass or bottle in a heated water bath to melt the wax, which can be poured out and stored for reuse or tossed as we see fit. At that point, the glass or bottle can be filled with a different color of gel wax. Removing all the gel wax can be challenging, so I do not recommend removing gel wax and then trying to use the vessel or bottle for actual consumable liquids afterward.

Working with Gel wax is fairly easy and similar to working with candle wax. We use a separate pan for gel wax, so the material remains transparent (not mixing with opaque candle wax). Gel wax does tend to smoke if it is heated up too much, so watch the temperature and ensure you have good ventilation. We melt the wax then add the colorant and stir until it is well combined; then we pour it into the bottle or glass we need to be filled. As mentioned above, you can rotate the object so the wax evenly coats the outer surface but doesn't fill the entire vessel; you just need to keep rotating it evenly until the wax cools and solidifies. After we have filled all the vessels we need with the wax we let the rest cool in the pan. We can then scrape it out and store it in a Zip-lock bag with a date and a label on it so we know what color it is and what show it was made for.

64 IMAGE TRANSFER METHODS

We often need to transfer an image onto a surface, and much like aging paper, there are many methods out there. Here are a few:

a. T-shirt transfer sheets – We have been using this for a long time, and it works well. Often, we need to make period-looking documents, but they want to hold up for a long run (20–40 performances).

In these cases, using paper is not always the best choice as they will need to be replaced regularly. So, we often switch to fabric for these documents, but we want them to look similar to the paper documents we create, so we want the text to be printed in an appropriate font. Running fabric directly through a printer is not always the most convenient or appropriate thing to do. We purchase t-shirt transfers and use those. We print the text onto the T-shirt transfer (reminder to read instructions carefully as some of these products require you to mirror the text because of how they get ironed onto the fabric, while others do not). Once we have printed the text on the transfers, we follow the directions provided with the transfers and iron them onto a piece of fabric. We generally use a lightweight muslin but can use a canvas or a beige sheet, depending on the look we are going for. Once ironed on and cooled, we can treat the fabric similarly to the paper treatments discussed in this chapter's tip #59 to age/distress the document(s).

b. Waxed paper method – this method is interesting because we have successfully used it on many different substrates, including fabric, wood, and several plastics. I have not tried it on metal yet, but I feel it would also work there. You need to cut the waxed paper to the size you want to send through your printer. You can trace your paper size and cut out the waxed paper. If your image has lettering, you need to flip it so the wording will appear backward when it prints. It would be best to use an inkjet printer to make this work. Generally, it is easier to place a piece of paper into the printer to lay your waxed paper on top of so that you know the waxed paper is lined up in the machine correctly. Once it prints out, give it 30 seconds to 1 minute for the ink to dry on the waxed paper so it doesn't smear. You then flip your image onto the surface you want the image on, and using a stiff plastic applicator (like a credit card), you want to hold the waxed paper firmly and press the image onto your substrate.

c. Carbon paper – This has been around for a long time, but recently, I have found the artisans in my shop do not know about it. Carbon paper is a thin paper covered on one side with a thin layer of carbon or graphite (like what is in a pencil). We print out a copy of the image we want to transfer, grab some carbon paper, and are now ready to transfer the image. We determine where we want the image to be on the object and tape a piece of carbon paper larger than the image over that area with the carbon side facing the object. We then tape the image on top of that. We then take a sharp pencil or a pen and trace the image; as we do so, the carbon is transferred from the carbon paper to your object. Once we are done tracing, we remove the image and the carbon paper; there is a line drawing of everything we traced in carbon. We then often pencil or marker the lines to solidify the image on the object. If you cannot find carbon paper you can make your own. First, print the image you want to transfer on a piece of paper. Flip the paper over and rub/cover the back of the piece of paper with graphite, making the graphite covered area slightly larger than your printed image on the front. We generally use a graphite stick bought from an art supply store. Once you have covered the area where your image is then flip the paper over and place it on your substrate. Trace the lines as you would with carbon paper and when you lift off the piece of paper the image will have transferred.

d. Projection — when dealing with image transfers on large objects, I find one of the best ways to do this is with a projector. We have multiple different projector types, and depending on how the initial image is provided will help determine which projector might be suitable for the job. We have a standard school overhead projector, which would require the image to be on a transparent acetate sheet. We also have an opaque projector where the image can be on any opaque surface. We slide the image in and focus it, and the image is projected onto the surface we want to copy it onto. The drawback of these two types of projectors is that to change the size of the projected image, we either need to physically move the projector or the surface we are projecting on, so it can take a bit of maneuvering to get the image exactly the size we need without a lot of adjustment and futzing. Also, the area we are working in needs to be pretty dark for the details in the image to show on the projected surface. You should also be aware of keystoning (when the projector distorts/warps the image due to not being perpendicular to the centerline of the object being projected on). The plus is we don't need any "technology" to project images using these methods. Today's more common option is to use a digital projector that can hook up to a laptop, computer, tablet, or phone to project the image. Depending on the projector's lumens, darkening the work area might not be necessary. If the scale is not quite right, we can adjust the image size on the technology without moving the projection surface or the projector around too much. Also, if we find we need to adjust the image, that can happen on the fly in the technology rather than having to print out a new image with the more arcane technologies mentioned earlier. I will say that we use all these different methods depending on the complexity of the image, the space available, and the particulars of the project we are faced with.

e. Pounce and chalk or graphite – The pounce wheel is another traditional method – when a projector is unavailable. This handheld device has a rotating wheel on the end that has little needle-like projections around the edges of the wheel. As it is rolled, it pokes small holes through paper. (It is essential for the life of the pounce wheel to always pounce on a soft surface, not to destroy the sharpness of the tips). We often pounce on a piece of ridged foam – Styrofoam or insulating foam, though homosote or cork would also work as a surface. Pouncing generally works well with large images – it is often used in scenic art to transfer very large graphic shapes onto drops or walls. We lay the printed or drawn illustration on the "soft" substrate, and using the pounce wheel, we trace over the lines of the image, making sure to apply enough pressure that we are piercing through the paper the image is on. Once we are done tracing, we take the "pounce" – the image with the tiny holes in it and attach it with tape to the object we want to transfer it to. Once secure, we then use a pounce bag (a semi-sheer fabric bag that is filled with either powdered chalk or charcoal) and gently tap the image, following the lines, to allow some of the chalk or graphite to penetrate the holes the pounce wheel has made leaving residue on the final image surface. Once the whole image has been pounce bagged, we remove the paper pounce, and the image should be on the object as a series of dots. Depending on how we plan to finish the picture, we might use a pencil or marker to connect the dots and make the image more solid before completing the work. Once the image has been traced onto the object, we often use a rag or a flogger to flog off the dust from the chalk or the charcoal so it does not interfere with the finishes.

f. Acetone – We have only used this for wood transfer a few times, as I learned about it recently. Also, it is a bit more caustic than many of the other methods we have discussed in this tip, but it does work well for the given circumstance. This works best with laser-printed or copied images (heat set toner rather than ink). As with the wax paper method, if our image has text, we must flip it before printing it. Once we have a copy or a paper print of the image, we lay it toner side down onto our substrate, then wearing gloves, we brush acetone over the paper (Be careful not to use too much, or the image will spread and get fuzzy). We use just enough to make the paper wet. Once the entire image has been covered, we wait a few seconds and then pull up the paper image. The original image should have transferred to the substrate. Once it has dried, the transferred image needs to be sealed to protect it from damage.

g. Water-based poly transfers – we put a thin layer of water-based poly on our substrate (we move sort of quickly as we want it to be wet when we apply our toner image (copy)), like the acetone transfer; this works best with copied or laser printed images. Once the substrate is covered with polyacrylic, we lay our image face down in the polyacrylic and push from the center out in all directions to ensure we have good adhesion and no air bubbles. We then set it aside to dry for roughly one hour. Once it is dry, we get some water and a stiff toothbrush or other stiff scrubbing brush that is not too abrasive. We wet the paper slightly and peeled it up as much as possible, then slowly work up any paper still adhered to the substrate using the stiff brush. We keep working until all the paper is removed. What is left is a good-quality copy of the original image on the substrate. The same idea works with Liquitex Gel Medium or Modge Podge. These are a thicker gel, so it tends to hold on to the paper more and make it hard to clean off, but the results will be similar if cleaned up well.

65   PUFF CIGARETTES

A decent amount of shows require smoking onstage. Generally, establishing the idea with a few puffs on the smoking device will allow the audience to buy in. Then, the actor can dispose of the smoking product appropriately, and the action can continue. Many actors and theaters are banning the use of cigarettes, herbal or otherwise, in productions, and many states also ban them in public places. However, some states are exempting theatrical use; Utah is not one of those states. Thus, the industry started switching to e-smoke products, which seemed to solve many of our problems; we have learned more over the last decade and know that even 0 nicotine products are unhealthy for people. When Utah passed its public smoking ban, it went so far as to ban the use of any e-cig type product when it put the ban in place and did not include an exemption for theatrical use (this, of course, occurred right after we invested nearly $1,000 in e – pipes cigars and cigarettes).

Shows still require the use of cigarettes, pipes, blunts, etc. We occasionally use commercially available Puff-Puff cigarettes, but they don't fit every need as they have a distinct look that sets them in a specific period. We have developed a system for creating our own puff cigarettes, pipes, etc. If making a cigarette, blunt, or cigar, we begin with a straw cut to the length of our finished smoking product. We fill the straw 7/8 of the way with fiber fill or cotton batting; don't jam it in as you want air to flow through it. We then fill the remaining portion with cornstarch. We make a metal mesh cap and slide it over the end with the cornstarch. Once that is complete, we wrap the outside of the straw with material to the size and shape of the finished smoking product so it looks appropriate. If we have a long run, we might make it so the straw can be removed and refilled, or we will make several units so when one starts to not "puff" as well, it can be discarded and a new one used. We have also fitted up some of our pipes with some cornstarch, a bit of batting, and a small metal screen to give a realistic pipe-smoking effect.

We then train the actors to only blow gently to create little puffs of smoke. We warn them not to suck, as it will cause them to inhale some cornstarch which will cause coughing and dry out the performer's mouth. We sell it to the audience by teaching the actors to go through the lighting ritual. They light a match or lighter as if they were lighting the cigarette or cigar, but while not actually getting the fire near the fake cigarette, we often have them mask this bit with their hand as if there is a draft in the room so they need to protect the flame. Then they take a few puffs (blowing out, which is the opposite of actual smoking) on the cigarette or cigar, make the audience buy into the smoking, and then move on with stage business and not dwell on the smoking. It reads well and is believable for a little bit, but if it continued for a long time, the willing suspension of disbelief of the audience would creep in and ruin the illusion.

Specialized tools of the trade
Seven

Over the years, we have found many specialized tools and equipment created for other industries that have served us well in the props department. Many of these machines or devices can be a bit cost-prohibitive, so we often wait until we have a show where they will really help us reduce time or energy, and we use the show budget and some supply/tool money to purchase the equipment, adding it to our arsenal of items we can use in the future to solve various prop issues that arise. You don't need to own these to be successful in props; a good pair of scissors, a hot glue gun, and some imagination will go a long way to making you successful in props. Knowing these tools/equipment exist and how they could be helpful on particular projects is good information to have. You might find someone in your area who has one of these devices or tools and would be willing to loan or rent them to you if you need them for a particular project.

Below are some examples of those machines/devices/equipment, examples of how they have been used at the Utah Shakespeare Festival, and some general information about the equipment being discussed. There are many things out there that we need to be aware of, and I am continually on the lookout for new gadgets and equipment that might have a good use in the prop world. I sometimes hear that some of these tools and devices take the artistry out of what we do; using the machines to create a statue or cut out intricate molding takes away from the hand-built nature of scenery or props. I understand the point, but they are tools that, if used correctly, can enhance the product by providing finer and more accurate detail in less time, allowing the artisans more time to focus on the fit and finish of a piece.

66 SPLIT RING PLIERS

For a production of *Shakespeare in Love*, the designer designed a series of ten candelabras that he wanted to be used throughout the show. The

DOI: 10.4324/9781003384182-7

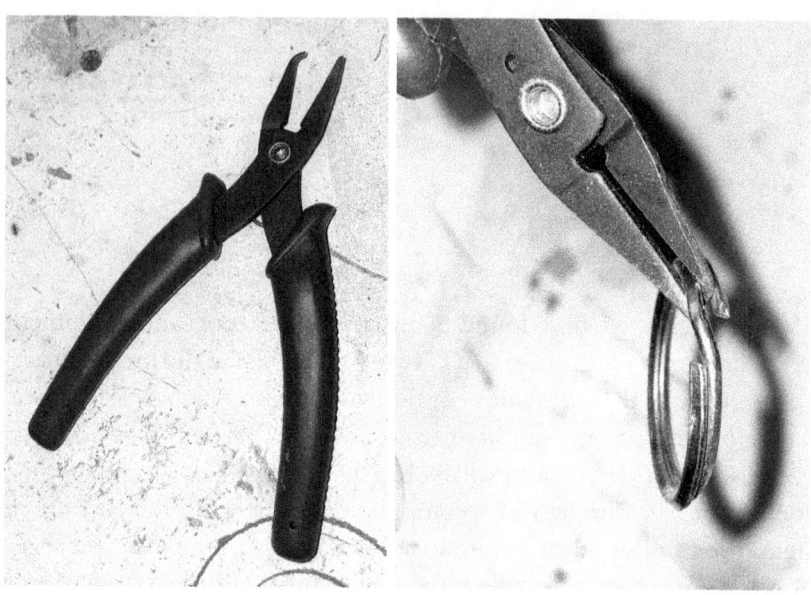

Image 7.1 Two photos showing a pair of split ring pliers (left) and the pliers opening a split ring (right).
Source: Photos by the author.

research image he sent us was of a chandelier and chandelier stand (so there were many swaged chains on the piece). There ended up being about 160 pieces of chain that needed to be attached to these candelabras. We learned the value of split ring pliers. (See Image 7.1.) They take a bit of getting used to, but they have a point on one side of the pliers that lifts part of the split ring and allows you to slide it onto something. It sped up the process immensely.

67 FRAME POINT DRIVER

This device (see Image 7.2) is similar to a stapler in its function but fires little arrow-shaped points parallel to the bottom of the driver. It is used in the art framing industry to hold in glass, mats, and artwork. This is the main thing we use it for as well. It speeds up the framing of art substantially, and the points are bendable, so if you need to switch out artwork, you do not necessarily need to remove them all to do so.

68 DREMEL QUICK-RELEASE TIPS

I don't often recommend specific products, but I love the Dremel quick-release grinding discs and sanding drums. We use those two

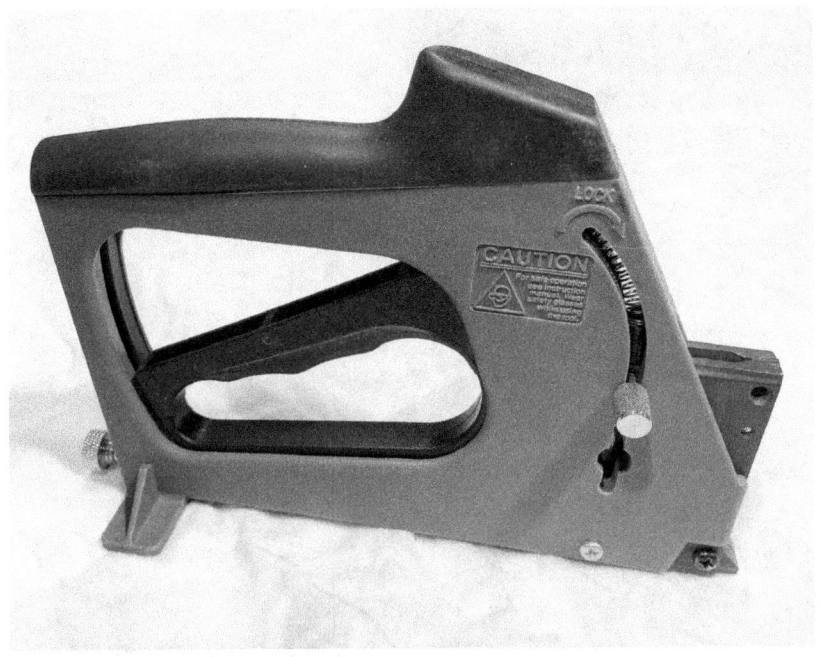

Image 7.2 A photo of a frame point driver.
Source: Photo by the author.

Dremel attachments nearly every day in the shop, and the fact that they have created a quick-release method so you can change out the grinding disc or sanding drum in seconds speeds up the process and makes the workflow better.

69 CHAIN BUSTING PLIERS

This pair of pliers (see Image 7.3) is amazing when working with chain. The pliers are spring-loaded and when you put them into a link of chain and squeeze they force the link of chain to open up allowing you to split the chain into parts or to add something to the chain (a clip, a hanging ring for a light fixture, etc.) The pliers also allow you to close back up the chain by putting the open link on the lower part of the handle, when pressure is applied to link is forced closed.

70 FLORAL STEMMING MACHINE

We make a lot of hedges and topiary at the Utah Shakespeare Festival. Over the years, we have done many different things to achieve these

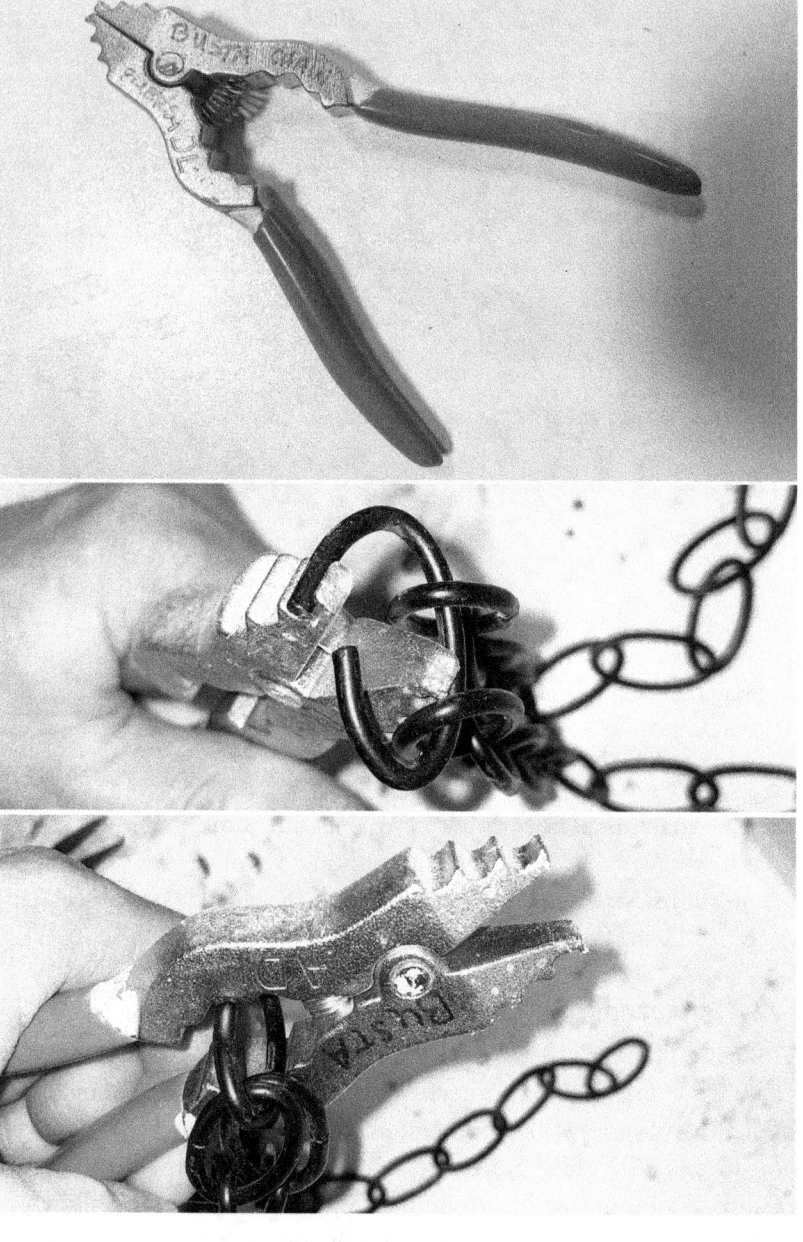

Image 7.3 Photos showing chain busting pliers (top), the pliers breaking a link of chain (middle), and closing a link of chain (bottom).

Source: Photos by the author.

floral creations, but the best thing we have found is using picks of greenery or floral to cover large areas quickly with a uniform covering. A "pick" is a small piece of greenery or floral with a slightly barbed end designed to be pushed into a substructure (usually foam) to cover that substructure with greenery or floral. You can purchase individual picks of boxwood, ivy, etc., to make hedges or topiaries. Still, since the company does all the prep work for you, it can get expensive fairly quickly, especially if your hedge or topiary is of any substantial size. The alternative is to buy a floral stemming machine and create the picks yourself from raw chunks of artificial floral and greenery. You can purchase new artificial greenery, or we have found that over time, our foliage sheds parts, so in the bottoms of many of our floral bins are little random pieces of greenery that we can use to create our own picks using the stemming machine.

Now, more specific information about the machine. (See Image 7.4.) A new machine will set you back $250–450, but I have found tons of used machines online for under $100. The picks/barbs are also inexpensive, running about $30 for 2,000. The machine has a heavy cast iron base with a crank handle on the side, and in the middle is a structure that allows you to place the metal barbs within it; there is a weight you slide on top of the barbs to make sure they slide down the column with each crank of the handle.

You load the machine with the barbs and are ready to start producing picks. To do this, you cut the greenery or floral to length, then crank the handle in one direction, and the barb slides into place at the end of the machine. You lay the back end (the non-floral end, the end that is just a straight piece of plastic or wire) of your greenery or floral onto the top of the barb and crank the handle the rest of the way. As you do this, little arms squeeze the sides of the metal barb around your floral piece and pressure fit them together. Make sure to crank the handle all the way so that the pressure forces the metal barb and the plastic greenery together in a tight fashion. Once that is done, you pull out your greenery, and it now has a barbed metal piece attached to the end, allowing you to apply it to your substructure and create your floral or greenery masterpiece – one small warning: the barbs are sharp; so be careful when handling or storing them. (See Image 7.5 to see the barbs attached to greenery pieces.)

Image 7.4 A photo of the Festival's stemming machine.
Source: Photo by the author.

71 DIE-CUTTING MACHINE

A die-cutting machine uses a sharp metal blade in the shape of an object (the die) to cut that shape out of fabric, paper, or similar materials. They are very popular in scrapbooking and quilting. For a production of *A Midsummer Night's Dream* in 2011, the Festival's 50th anniversary season, the designer had this idea about making a huge weeping willow on stage. He wanted semi-transparent leaves made of multiple shades of green fabric. After some research, we purchased an AccuQuilt die-cutting machine. We paid for a custom die (with three identical leaves on it). We could stack eight to ten layers of sheer fabric and run the stack through the machine (it is a hand crank). With the

Image 7.5 A photo showing pieces of greenery with picks attached to them.

Source: Photo by the author.

three-leaf die, we cut about 30 leaves per pass. It took a while, but we eventually cut 40,000 leaves on the machine. We then used quilt/price tagging guns to attach the leaves to dyed twill tape, which was attached to the metal and wood armature scenery made for the tree arms (Image 7.6).

We have also purchased a custom Fleur-di-Lis die, which we have used on multiple occasions to make French banners and flags for numerous productions. They also have many stock dies and add more regularly, which we have added to our collection over the years. A leaf die to make blood-red oak leaves, which fell from the heavens during every murder in *MacBeth*. We used a heart die with red felt to make heart garlands for *The Marvelous Wonderettes*, flowers for multiple flower drops, and a flying flower wall for Bohemia in *The Winter's Tale*. They specifically say that their machine is only for fabric, which works on everything from lightweight sheers to dense upholstery fabric.

Image 7.6 A photo of Ben Charles as Puck in the Utah Shakespeare Festival's 2011 production of A Midsummer Night's Dream. Scenic design by Bill Forrester; lighting design by Donna Ruzika; costume design by Janet L. Swenson.

Source: Copyright Utah Shakespeare Festival. Photo by Karl Hugh.

We have also successfully cut tissue paper, typing paper, construction paper, and felt with the dies (Image 7.7).

72 GROMMET SETTER/RIVET SETTER/BUTTON MAKER

Grommet machines come in several types and sizes. Our shop has three different tabletop models, while our costume craft department has a foot-powered unit that is a bit larger and more industrial. The grommet machine, while mechanical (no motor), does allow for quicker and quieter application of grommets and rivets into multiple materials and quickly makes fabric-covered buttons for upholstery projects.

Each machine slightly differs in how you insert the grommet or rivet, but all follow the same basic principles. You punch a hole in the fabric slightly smaller than the size of the grommet or rivet you want to install. Then, you install the dies for the size of the grommet or rivet. Each size has its own set of dies, so you will spend a bit of money on

Image 7.7 A photo of our AccuQuilt die-cutting machine.
Source: Photo by the author.

these, but you can build up your collection over time as new sizes are needed for projects. Once the dies are installed in the machine, you place half the grommet on the lower die, then insert your fabric with your precut hole. You put the top part of the grommet on the pile, and then make sure your top die is either attached to the machine or placed on top of the pile, depending on the exact nature of your machine. You then exert a decent amount of force and push the arm of the machine down, which compresses the multiple pieces of your grommet or rivet and, due to the nature of the dies, curls the metal around and locks itself together while encasing your fabric layer(s) in between. You must apply enough pressure so the grommet or rivet is entirely "set" and not loose on the fabric. We often bolt our machine down to a non-rolling table and make sure it sits low enough that you can apply a good amount of body pressure to allow for a proper set.

With the switching out of dies, this machine can also make fabric-covered buttons for upholstery in much the same way. First, you need to cut out pieces of fabric in circles that are the correct size. Each set of dies comes with a cutter and two die components. We use a piece of hardwood as our base, lay our fabric on the hardwood, and then lay the cutter on top with the sharp edge touching the material. One of our grommet machines has a flat plate you can apply to the arm, and with the body pressure when pushing the arm down, you will cut through the fabric and make the circle you need. Once that is completed for the number of buttons you need (always make a few extras!), you are ready to assemble your buttons. You begin by placing the lower die in the machine, putting your fabric circle over the die, and pushing the front of the button into the fabric. It then slides into the lower die, and the fabric edges should stand up around it. You then place the back of the button in the upper die and put it on top of the lower die. When you apply downward pressure, the fabric curls inside the front of the button, and the back of the button pushes down on the fabric. The die crimps the front of the button around the back, pinning the fabric edges inside the button, squeezing all the parts together, and "setting" the button. So, when it is removed from the machine, it is a single unit with the fabric covering the front with all edges tucked in, and the back flat and smooth and ready to be applied to your costume or in the world of props to be used for button tufted upholstery (see more information in Chapter Four, Tip 37) (Image 7.8).

73 VACUUM FORMER MACHINE

The vacuum former machine heats plastic to a temperature where it is malleable, and then that plastic is placed over an object, a vacuum pump is turned on and sucks the air out from between the heated plastic and the original object making a duplicate of that object. The machine comprises three main parts: a heating element, a vacuum table, and a plastic sheet frame. The plastic is placed and locked into the frame. Once that is completed, you move the plastic to the heating section of the machine, and you begin to heat the plastic (you need to watch the plastic carefully as you don't want it to overheat, which can cause it to burn or melt holes in the plastic making it unusable). While it is heating, you can lay the object(s) you want to "copy" onto the vacuum table. Once the plastic is heated to the correct level of malleability, you swing or lower the plastic from the heating element to the vacuum table. As the plastic settles over the objects on the table, you turn on the vacuum which will suck all the air out from under the plastic and around the objects you have placed there and make a thin plastic shell replica of the original item. It is a rapid process, and you don't want to

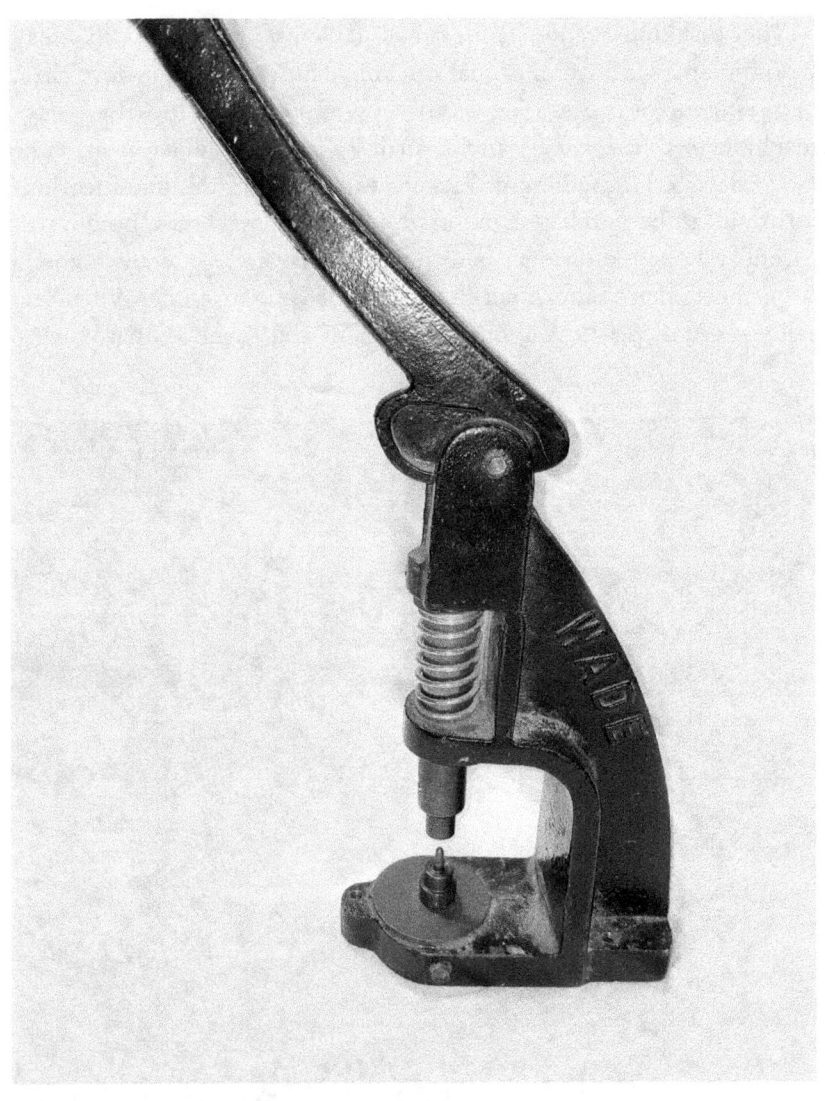

Image 7.8 A photo of one of our grommet setting machines.
Source: Photo by the author.

give the plastic a chance to cool down before you vacuum the air out. Once the shapes are set, you will want to provide the plastic with some time to cool before removing the sheet from the machine. Be aware of your original objects and be careful that they do not fall out of the plastic and fall to the ground, possibly damaging them.

The machines range from small tabletop versions with small working areas to machines that can run a full 4-foot by 8-foot sheet of plastic in one pass. The Festival owns both a 4-foot by 4-foot machine (see Image 7.9) and a small 12" by 18" tabletop machine (see image 7.11). Different thicknesses of plastics designed for heat forming can be purchased and used with these machines, both transparent and opaque varieties in different colors. They generally come in large sheets that you can cut to the size of your machine. When you call your local plastics supplier, make sure you mention that you are

Image 7.9 A photo of the larger vacuum form machine we own.
Source: Photo by the author.

vacuum-forming these plastics, you want to ensure the plastics you get don't smoke or off gas chemicals when heated and that they will soften, form well, and not crack or break when cooled.

This old-school method of duplication is slowly going out of style, as it is being replaced by 3-D printing, CNCs, and molding and casting. However, I still find it super beneficial due to the copy's lightness and the duplicate's quick creation. The larger machines can also make large-scale pieces that would be very hard to make in a 3-D printer or with a mold. Our costume crafts department makes base layers for helmets and breastplates out of the plastic. We have produced multiple types of footlights (Clamshell, ½ can, etc.) and a multi-tier jiggly Jell-O prop for a clown to carry across the stage for a play a few years ago. The scenery department has used the machine to create four-foot brick sections for walls and multiple types of column tops for various shows. Many years ago, we had a designer who wanted a 3-D carved oversized vine patterned molding for a large table that would have taken a long time to carve by hand and was not commercially available. We had an artisan create a three foot section of it and made multiple copies with the machine in a couple of hours. We were able to wrap the entire table with this very custom molding in short order.

A few words about the items you are casting: to create good copies with this technology, the piece needs to have a flat back and almost no undercuts (or it will be tough to remove from the plastic without tearing the sheet). Sometimes, this means you must add some clay or other substance to help make the object work for the machine. Making a plaster cast (or a few if you have a larger machine) will help make the molding process easier. Also, if your original item has a lot of deep detail, you might need to drill some holes through it to allow the vacuum to successfully get the air sucked out of all areas and create a good impression of the object details. As you begin process, some experimentation helps ensure a good copy with every machine pass (Images 7.10).

74 LARGE FORMAT PRINTER

A large format printer accepts materials from 18" to 100" wide and can print on many substrates in both sheet and roll form, depending on the machine. They often have more ink options than standard

Image 7.10 A photo of samples of items we have formed on our machine.

Source: Photo by the author.

printers, including UV-stable inks. We have had a 44" Canon machine for nearly 15 years. Due to its outdated software (it is having compatibility issues with our computer operating systems), we have decided to replace it with a new machine. The original machine has been a workhorse for us.

If you are looking into this type of machine, I highly recommend getting one that will do roll and sheet feed and allow you to put multiple substrates through the machine. Numerous companies make fabric rolls that can be fed through these machines, everything from sheers to thin velvets. We regularly run canvas and cotton poplin through our machine. It is essential to have a device that will handle fabrics and still be gentle enough to run newsprint or vellum through it when you need to make newspapers or translucent stained-glass panels.

We often print on fabrics. We do many "paintings" on canvas, both completed artworks to be framed and hung on sets and works-in-progress that performers are "painting" on stage. We have printed custom fabric panels for large dressing screens and printed a backdrop in sections to be wrapped around foam-core boards and fit into the wall sections of our outdoor theater. We regularly print fabric maps and scrolls. We ran over 500 feet of Tyvek through it a few years ago to print 200 sheets of Shakespeare's folio pages to hang around our outdoor theater for The Book of Will, then found out the Tyvek was too noisy in the wind and reprinted most of those pages on muslin to make them quieter. We used the Tyvek onstage for other scenes where the wind would not buffet it around. I have never told the costume department that we could print custom fabric in-house because that is all the machine would be doing.

We also print many graphics on sticky back vinyl (essentially making our own stickers) of nearly any size to give a photo-realistic look to clock faces, logos for appliances, and the like. We also use it to make custom record sleeves, calendars, cereal boxes, etc. We have printed wallpaper for the scenic department. We also use it to print full-scale patterns and pounces, sometimes in multiple pieces that need to be taped together. Last year, scenery built and painted a 12' stained glass

Image 7.11 A photo of our small table top vacuum form machine.
Source: Photo by the author.

window for *The Sound of Music*, and we printed all the pounces on our machine. We print dozens of newspapers nearly every year as well.

Over its lifespan, our printer has saved us tens of thousands of dollars, as we have been able to print in-house versus having to job all of these projects out to printing companies. Particularly as the shows evolve, we need to reprint or adjust things based on the rehearsal process. It is useful to multiple departments, not just production. Ensure your company establishes a protocol for paying for the machine's maintenance and supplies (ink, paper, fabrics). Props generally gets stuck buying new ink (roughly $300 a pop) or paper because we use it the most. With our machine upgrade, we are establishing a per printed foot cost so departments can pay into a fund that will cover maintenance and supplies when the needs arise in the future.

When investing in this type of machine, there are a few things to consider. Think about all the departments that might find it useful. Consider where the machine will be set up (dusty shop environments are not ideal for all the delicate electronics and moving parts.) and how big a machine is practical for your organization. As we looked at new machines, I was offered the option to upgrade to a 60" wide machine, but I could only think of two or three instances in 15 years where I had to seam something together from smaller pieces that would have made the larger machine worthwhile. So, we opted to go with a newer 44" machine and get backup ink and maintenance supplies with the initial order. This machine can be super helpful to multiple departments and is a sound investment that will pay for itself many times over, and if well taken care of, can last for a really long time (Image 7.12).

Basic knowledge of G-code machines

The following four machines all use similar technologies to accomplish their tasks. I will give you the essential information here so that in each section, I can talk about the specific machines' details and how they benefit props. For each of the devices below, you are manipulating a graphic of some sort within a computer program that is specific (proprietary) to the machine type you own. Once you have manipulated the graphic in the way you want, you are ready to send the information to the machine for processing. The software you used to create the image/graphic/3-d model takes that information and turns it into computer code that tells the device where

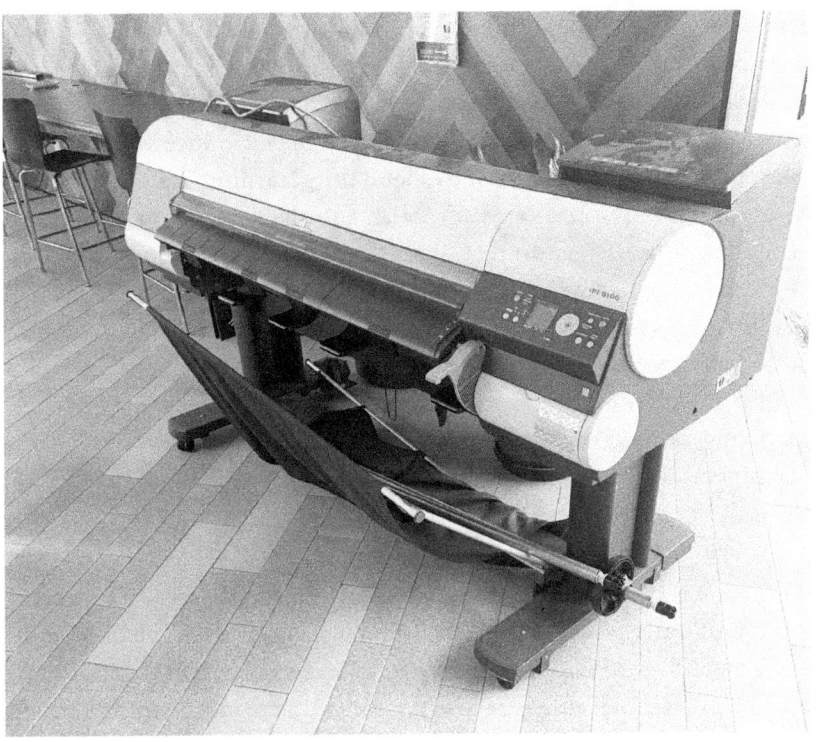

Image 7.12 A photo of our wide format printer.
Source: Photo by the author.

in space (x, y coordinates) or, in the case of CNC and 3D printing (x, y, z coordinates) you want to start the process on the material you have chosen, and what path the machine will follow. This path is known as a "tool path," which is the trajectories the cutting tool or 3D printer head follows during the machining process. The software generates the coordinate locations that the tool will follow. It sends those coordinates to the machine in question in the machining process. It follows those coordinates to cut out or build up your material until the object is complete.

Once you know the basics of each piece of software, you can explore and test the limits of your machine. Almost all manufacturers of these types of machines have great websites with tutorials and example videos. I have also found that most machines have tons of videos on YouTube or other online places for you to see what others are using the machines to create. This is a great way to learn more about the machines and their capabilities and will also inspire you on new and exciting ways these pieces of technology can enhance your ability to tell stories. One of the most significant things to be aware of when working with these machines is that they produce what you ask them to produce, so you need to spend time learning the software and being precise in your computer work and the calibration and set-up of the machine. If you do that, your chances of successful production increase dramatically. All of these machines have quirks that can trip you up and tricks that can help you produce better results. Some of these you can only learn by doing the work and experimenting. Still, I cannot stress enough watching online tutorials, reading reviews, and following others' project examples to really get to understand your machine(s) and its capabilities.

75 VINYL CUTTER

We have had a home/crafter vinyl cutting machine for a few years at our shop, but we recently had a little bit of budget left at the end of a season and were able to upgrade to a larger, more commercial/professional machine with a 24" bed. We use this machine mostly to cut vinyl (heat transfer and regular) and stencil material to make stencils for various painting projects. This is just the tip of the iceberg on what this and machines like it can do. They now make thin wood veneers that this machine can cut (so you could make intricate marquetry patterns for application to tables or the like). You can cut thin fabrics, thin cork material, thick cardstocks, and various other materials.

Here are a few examples of things we have used our machine for recently. We cut a metallic vinyl to create a gun manufacturer's logo to apply to a wood case we had built for a pair of dueling pistols needed for a duel sequence in a production. We used heat transfer vinyl (HTV) to make Roman emblems for flags and banners in a production of *Julius Caesar*. We also used heat transfer vinyl to mimic the look of silk-screened posters for a university logo in a production of *Thurgood*. We made flag elements (a star, a stripe, etc.) and applied them to both sides of flags for a production of *Coriolanus*. Several of these projects mimic the process of silk-screening discussed in Chapter Five, Tip 48; however, due to their one-off nature, using the heat transfer vinyl has proven to be a faster and more cost-effective way of achieving these items. Other prop people have used similar machines to make graphic book covers, lightweight box templates, etc.

There are many brands of machines, all with different features and options; I will not try to sell you on a specific brand. You should look for a machine that allows a lot of flexibility and options of materials it can process and the ability to import and manipulate multiple types of artwork within the machine's software. Several companies have proprietary graphic types, so you are limited in what you can do with the artwork. We found a machine that allows us to import many kinds of artwork, jpg, PSD, AI, etc. Once you have imported the graphic into the program, you have multiple options for manipulation; you can resize, rotate, duplicate, merge, flip, etc. Some software programs even allow you to build the graphic from scratch within the program itself. Due to the nature of prop work, I often try to reproduce a logo or a symbol that exists in the world, so importing something close to my final product speeds up the process. Once you have the graphic (either created or imported) to the size and details you want, then it is time to convert it into a "tool path" in our machine software that requires that you trace the object using a "trace function," which can then be saved for future use. You then load the machine with the appropriate material to cut and send the information from your computer to the vinyl cutter for it to cut out your object. I know we have just scratched the surface of what this machine can do for our shop, and I look forward to exploring the possibilities (Image 7.13).

76 3D PRINTER

3D printers use computer-aided design to create three-dimensional objects through a layering method. It involves layering materials, primarily types of plastics, to create objects. The basic machine layout is a bed on which the object is made and a gantry over the bed that moves a nozzle on the X, Y, and Z planes. As the nozzle moves, the computer code tells the nozzle when to dispense the product and when not to. The 3D printer is becoming a more common tool in the prop shop, and as technology continues to move forward, I think it will become essential for us in the future.

We are a little behind the times and have just purchased a machine. (We haven't printed anything yet, but it will happen in the next month

Image 7.13 A photo showing one of our vinyl cutting machines.
Source: Photo by the author.

or two.) While I need to learn more about this tool and the myriad ways it can help us create excellent props, others have had them for a while and have found many ways to make them useful in their prop shops. Some examples I know have happened over the last few years in shops around the country include printing a breakaway vase (for *Mary Poppins*) that had spaces for magnets to be epoxied in so that the vase could be reassembled after each performance. This would replace the idea of the greenware vases I discussed in Chapter Six. Another theater was able to use some software to take multiple photos of an actor's face and then turn that into a 3-D image, which they could print to make a decapitated head for a show (instead of having to do a life cast of the performer). Yet another theater recreated some small decorative elements on a vintage chandelier for which parts were no longer available. Beyond printing props or parts of props, other theaters have used the machines to print small parts to repair tools, create a unique hardware solution needed for a specific issue in a production, and make shop jigs and templates. I am excited to get our machine fired up and start exploring all the ways it will aid us in storytelling in the future (Image 7.14).

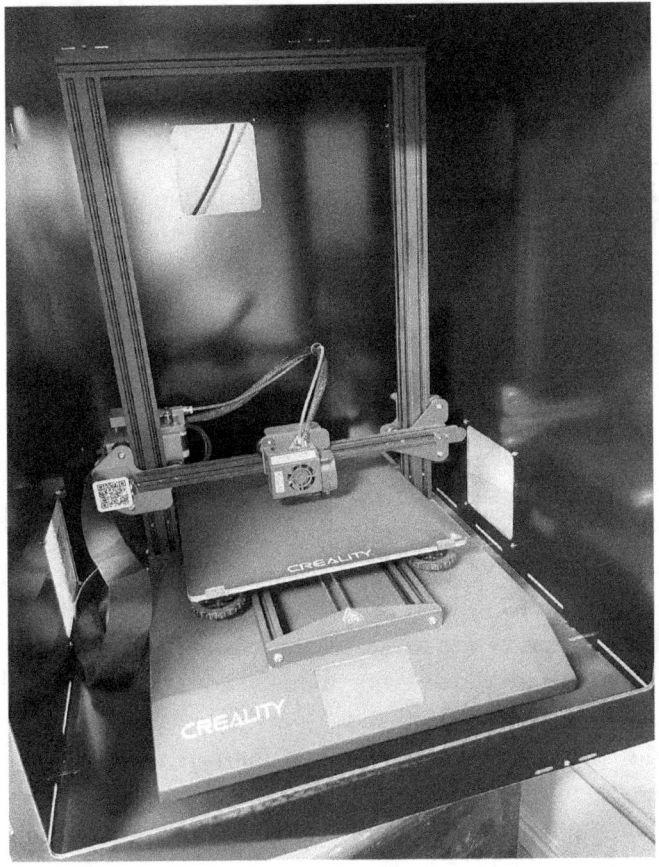

Image 7.14 A photo of our 3-D printer.
Source: Photo by the author.

77 LASER ENGRAVER/CUTTER

Another machine we have just purchased and are still exploring, but I know it will become super useful, is our laser engraver/cutter. Laser engraving/cutting is a process that uses a laser to vaporize (burn away) material. The size (wattage) of the laser and the substrate will determine if the material can be cut through with the laser or if it will etch/carve the surface. The intensity of the laser and the amount of passes the machine makes can be adjusted based on whether it is engraving or cutting and what the substrate is. Most machines come with a list of settings for common materials, and you can find additional information online. Once you have the machine set, you should test and verify the suggested settings work in your environment. Follow all safety instructions and be aware that the laser is burning things, so set it up in a safe location, ensure you have the proper ventilation, and always wear all the safety gear recommended by the machine manufacturer.

These machines have so many variables that you should consider how you think you will use it, where you can set it up, and how much you want to invest. We chose a machine that, with the extension kit, can engrave/cut an area roughly 20" by 40". It has a 20w laser and has some safety features built-in; we bought a vented enclosure for it and an air assist that blows compressed air on the surface immediately after the laser cuts to reduce burn marks and edge scorching. We also purchased a rotational tool allowing round or cylindrical objects to be engraved on the curved surface. These machines allow for so many substrates, with such repeatability and accuracy, that it will be great for many projects.

Our first planned project is some clock hands out of thin plastic that we will embed magnets into to allow a performer to rip the clock hands off the grandfather clock every night (70+ performances). We purchased fancy metal clock hands, but they are so thin and delicate that the actors bent them at one of the first rehearsals, so being able to cut them out of a slightly thicker plastic will still give us the look we want, but we will have a much more robust prop that will handle the abuse (Image 7.15).

78 CNC ROUTER

A CNC (computer numeric control) router works by moving a router or high-speed spindle to specific x, y, and z coordinates within the work area, then using the cutting tool to remove material. The machine can cut precise detail through multiple passes and even carve into woods, foams, and ferrous metals. This tool is becoming increasingly popular and common in scene and prop shops worldwide.

We have shared a machine with our university theater department for several years. The Festival's scene shop purchased an upgraded machine recently with a pneumatic hold-down system and a bit changer, which has sped up the workflow considerably. Over the last several years, we have done many standard 2-D type projects: fancy panels for the door of a grandfather clock, a frame for a very

Image 7.15 A photo of our laser engraver/cutter.
Source: Photo by the author.

ornate changing screen (which we have now made three times in different sizes), ornate pianoforte legs for *Sweeney Todd*, and the list goes on. For a production of *Guys and Dolls*, we took the logo of the Save-A-Soul Mission and carved out shields with the lettering on them to attach to several stock benches, making them feel very custom and specific to the production.

The great thing about this machine is that you can explore and find new things it can do for you. One of the things that the scenic art department has been doing is making sculptures with it. We have done five or six statues in the last several years. We often do multiple photos of the performer in the appropriate costume, then put those photos into software that creates a 3D image, which we then slice (often into 2" layers – but we can do 1" if the detail is needed) then using the CNC cut out each layer and glue them all together often with some internal metal or wood structure. The painters then spend some time smoothing edges and doing finishing work. It has cut the sculpting time to a ¼ of what it once was.

Recent projects include a three times size bust of an actor in the role of Julius Caesar, a lifelike replica of Pericles' daughter for *Pericles*, and two oversized statues (12'+ tall) of two Greek gods as the sides of an arched tree unit for a production of *Twelfth Night*. For our current season, the scene shop has put the machine into overdrive, cutting out fancy wood molding for *The Play That Goes Wrong*, multiple layers of an intricate fireplace unit for the same show, Ionic column capitals out of foam for *Jane Austen's Emma the Musical*, and oversized capitals also out of foam for a production of *A Midsummer Night's Dream*. We are excited to spend some time with the machine and start playing with its potential for more 3-D objects that we can use in future prop construction (Image 7.16).

Image 7.16 A photo of the set, Scenic design by Apollo Mark Weaver and lighting design by Michael Pasquini for the Utah Shakespeare Festival's 2019 production of Twelfth Night.
Source: Copyright Utah Shakespeare Festival. Photo by Karl Hugh.

Prop reference

Eight

In my opinion, one of the most fascinating things about props is the research. Due to the nature of the variety of shows, you get to find out all kinds of fun and interesting tidbits of knowledge that are very specific and, to some extent, arcane. I love finding out the right name for something or the reasoning behind a word (see Chapter Twelve for some excellent examples). The rabbit holes you can fall into when looking for an object or figuring out what a playwright meant when they used a specific word or phrase can be enlightening and entertaining. When doing research, it is important to know something about the source. The Internet has made research more accessible, but most sites are not fact-checked or peer-reviewed (anyone can put nearly anything on the internet, but that doesn't make it true or reliable). Books, dictionaries, and journals are reviewed and edited, so there is a trust factor that makes the information in them more reliable. I am not saying you can't do research on the internet or that everything you read there is false/fake, but just be aware of where your research is coming from and how factual it is.

79 CASK TERMINOLOGY

If you ever want to go down a crazy rabbit hole of arcane information, I suggest looking up information about cask sizes and terms; it is fascinating and wild. While the specifics of the cask's dimensions are minutia, knowing the gist of the sizes is helpful. Long ago, ale and beer were considered different drinks, so ale and beer cask sizes were slightly different, though with similar names. Wines also used the same names but had different dimensions. In the 1800s, England switched to the Imperial system of measurement, so the size of a gallon changed, while in America, the old size was still prevalent, which is why many of the volumes listed are a range. I also learned that the correct term is "cask" and that "barrel" is actually a particular size, though the term barrel is used almost exclusively in modern parlance. Again, all the details are a little less critical, but the scale of the casks compared to each other and a rough idea of the liquid capacity is helpful in the world of props. There are more cask types than I will cover here, but these are the main casks, their relative sizes, and some comparisons to each other that might prove helpful. Many of these come up in Shakespeare productions, which is why I even know about them.

a. Pin – 20 liters, a very small cask. It is nearly half a firkin (you will rarely, if ever, see a cask of this size).
b. Firkin – 41 liters, roughly a ¼ of a barrel, or half a kilderkin. (The name is derived from the Middle Dutch Derivative meaning "fourth".)
c. Octave – 50 liters, about a quarter the size of an American standard barrel.
d. Rundlet – 68 liters.
e. Kilderkin – 82 liters (from the Dutch for "small cask").
f. Quarter cask – 125 liters.
g. British barrel – 160 liter, also referred to as a tierce.
h. American standard barrel – 190–200 liters. This is the cask size and shape most often associated with the term barrel.
i. Hogshead – 230–250 liters. It is equal to a roughly a quarter tun or half a butt.
j. Barrique – 225–275 liters. It generally has a longer shape and is commonly used in the wine industry.
k. Pipe – about 350 liters. Like a Barrique, this barrel generally has a longer, thinner shape.
l. Puncheon – 450–500 liters. It is prevalent in the maturing of sherry. It's equal to about half a tun.
m. Butt/Drum – 600–650 liters. It is generally squatter and broader than many others.
n. Tun – about 1,150 liters. A cask double the size of a butt and equal to eight barrels.

80 DRINK GLASSES

Below are explanations and basic information on two dozen types of glassware. There are dozens more glass shapes and types than I will cover here; I found at least 22 different kinds of glasses for wines alone. This section aims to help you determine the best glass shape/ type for a given circumstance so that your audience is not drawn out of the production because of a wrong choice on your part. Most of the glass shapes directly correlate with the experience of drinking the particular drink that the glass is for, allowing for a more complete imbibing event. This list is not comprehensive in any way, but it is a good starting place for many of the drinking situations you will encounter in play production. I have numbered the glasses and have included a visual chart (see Image 8.1) that shows the shape of each of the glasses.

Cocktail glasses
1. Rocks glass – also known as a lowball or Old-fashioned glass. This is a short glass for drinking spirits "on the rocks" (over ice) or "neat" (just the liquor). This glass is short, making it suitable for muddling (the action or process of mixing a drink or stirring an ingredient into a drink) the ingredients for an Old-Fashioned Cocktail, which is mixed directly in the glass.
2. Double Old Fashioned – a glass slightly larger than a rocks or Old-fashioned glass but not twice the size as the name implies.
3. Highball glass – this is a tall version of the lowball. It is similar in size and style to a standard water glass. They are generally used for

Image 8.1 A chart of common drinking glasses with names. Can be enlarged to fit on an 8.5" × 11" piece of paper to be hung in the glassware section of your stock.

Source: Illustrations by the author.

cocktails with more ingredients or large amounts of juice or soda water. Drinks like Bloody Marys, Long Island ice teas, and mojitos are often served in these.

4. Collins glass – named specifically after the drink: The Tom Collins. This glass is similar to a highball glass but tends to be thinner, taller, and holds more liquid. The vertical sides prolong the carbonated bubbles of the soda water, which is a major ingredient in a Tom Collins. Also used for Mojitos and Whiskey Sours.
5. Irish coffee glass – It resembles a coffee mug on a stem, except it is made of glass instead of ceramic. Typically used for Irish coffee, which is a mix of coffee and whiskey (generally Irish – hence the name) and topped with whipped cream. This glass is also used for hot toddies and mulled cider.
6. Martini glass – The thin stem of this glass (and others) keeps the heat from your hands from warming up the liquid (drink). The flat angled side (typically relatively shallow) reduces the need to tip your head back to empty the glass. Generally used for Martinis, Manhattans, and Cosmopolitans.
7. Margarita glass – This glass has a bowl shape with a central indent; the shape is rumored to be modeled after a female breast. It is used almost exclusively for Margaritas.
8. Hurricane glass – this glass has a wide bottom, a narrow middle, and a flared lip, it was originally designed for the Hurricane cocktail but is now used for nearly all tropical drinks. The flared lip focuses the fruity aroma for the drinker and provides room for garnishes.
9. Snifter – the snifter is typically used for brandy; the round bowl shape allows the drinker to cradle the glass (slightly warming the contents). The narrower top opening allows the liquid's aroma to remain more trapped, allowing for a multi-sensory drinking experience. It is also used for beers with high alcohol content, as the shape captures the aromas and highlights the foam.
10. Cordial glass – a small wine glass-shaped vessel used for a small amount of liquid often served at the end of a meal.
11. Shot glass – holds just a small amount (typically four oz.) of liquid and is used almost exclusively for a single swallow of a straight liquor with no embellishments or ice.

12. Coupe – this class has a shallow broad bowl shape and was originally designed for champagne. The bubbles dissipate quickly due to the large surface area so it fell out of use for that liquid and is now often used for mixed drinks that are shaken with ice but poured without the cubes. The coupe glass is also popular for champagne; however, with its larger surface area, the bubbles dissipate faster, allowing the drink to go flat quicker.

Wine glasses

This covers the main types of wine glasses and a little about the purpose of the shapes. As a general rule, a standard pour of wine is generally 5 oz. With dessert wines, it is often 2–3 oz as they are sweeter and have higher alcohol content. Most wine glasses will look far from full with that size of pour, which is by design; the rest of the glass is there to release the aroma from the wine to enhance the drinking experience.

13. Flute (often referred to as a sparkling wine/champagne glass) – champagne glasses are typically upright with a narrow bowl that preserves the wine's carbonation and flavor. The smaller surface area controls the carbonation release, allowing more time to drink the liquid before it goes flat. This glass is generally small in size, so it helps with portion control, and due to the small amount of liquid if used for a toast, the wine would be consumed before the carbonation all dissipates. The flute is also used for cocktails at times but is most known for sparkling wine/champagne.
14. Red wine glasses – red wine glasses have some distinct features to enhance the taste of the wine. They are generally large with a round bowl and a big opening, which allows for enjoyment of the aroma of the wine. The larger surface area afforded the wine in this type of glass increases the oxidation rate, which smooths out the taste of red wines. Each type of glass has unique characteristics that enhance that particular style of red wine. Still, as described above, a standard red wine glass will work with nearly any red wine – a few specific red wine glasses include Bordeaux, Pinot Noir, Burgundy, and Cabernet Sauvignon.

15. White wine glass – white wine glasses are generally designed to focus more on preserving the wine's aroma than allowing it to breathe. The bowl is usually smaller than for red wines, is more u-shaped, and is more upright, both taller and narrower, than a typical red wine glass. The shape of these glasses also maintains the cooler temperature of the wine. White wine glasses typically have longer stems, keeping the warmth of the drinker's hand further from the bowl so as to not warm the wine. Some specialized glass types for whites include Chardonnay, Sauvignon Blanc, Montrachet, and Riesling.
16. Dessert wine glasses – typically, these glasses are substantially smaller than red or white glasses, allowing for smaller pours. Dessert wines tend to have a higher alcohol content and be sweeter, so less is needed. Port and sherry glasses are two common glass shapes for dessert wines.
17. Rose wine glasses – Rose wines have unique flavor profiles, and the glasses used to serve them often have a diamond shape or a softer bowl with a longer stem. The rim of the glass is the most critical part of the glass when it comes to rose wines, almost always having a flared or tapered lip.

Beer glasses

Beer glass shapes enhance the specific types of beer served in them in much the same way wine glasses serve specific wines. The shape, dimensions, and capacity of the glass allow it to elevate the aroma, taste, and color, as well as highlight the foam generation of the beverage. In general, high-fermentation beers are served in wider-mouthed glasses, while low-fermentation beers use thinner and longer glasses that favor effervescence. Again, there are dozens of varieties of beer glasses, and I am only covering some of the major shapes here.

18. Weizen glass – this glass is narrow at the bottom and widens at the top, which allows for control of the vast amount of foam that is formed with wheat beers. It is a taller glass which helps it capture the aroma of the beer.
19. Pilsner glass – This glass is tall, slender, and has a conical shape. They typically hold 12 ounces. This glass captures the effervescence and color of Pilsner beer.

20. Sling glass – The sling glass has a foot and tall tapered sides. It is used for a variety of cocktails and is also used to serve pilsner beer as the sling glass shape is similar to the pilsner glass.
21. Pint glass – This glass is ideal for the drinking of stout. It has a large mouth which provides a good layer of foam and facilitates drinking. It is ideal for beers that do not drink very cold or carbonated. They often have a bulge about an inch from the top, which helps prevent them from sticking together when stacked. This is referred to as a nonic bulge.
22. Beer mug – these are sturdy, with a thick wall. They have a large capacity and a handle that prevents the heat of the hand from cooling the beer. They are often used to drink English ale or stouts.
23. Tulip Glass – a curved glass (similar in shape to a tulip) that captures the aromatic qualities of beer, while its tight mouth allows for the formation of a dense layer of foam. It pairs well with beers with intense flavor and high alcohol content.
24. Stein – is a vessel traditionally made from ceramic or stoneware and having a lid. These were used to keep insects (particularly flies) from getting into the beer and also to keep the beer cold for an extended period of time. Metal steins with and without lids are also popular.

81 WINE BOTTLES

While researching some of the glasses above, I came across some information about wine bottles that was very interesting to me. The color and shape of the bottle will generally tell you the type of wine it contains. I was unaware of this and had always just grabbed a wine bottle off the bottle cart whenever we needed one. But now, knowing this information, I will be more aware of what wine the play calls for and which bottle I pull for that scene to allow for more authenticity in the storytelling.

There are literally hundreds of variations on wine bottles, but most fall into six basic shapes and a few basic colors. Generally, all red wines and champagne are served from darker green or brown bottles, which protect the wine from light, preventing oxidation. In contrast, white and rose wines tend to be in lighter green, amber, or clear bottles where you can see the liquid inside. White wines are generally served when they are younger, and they often store in the refrigerator, both of which help reduce oxidation.

six main wine bottle shapes

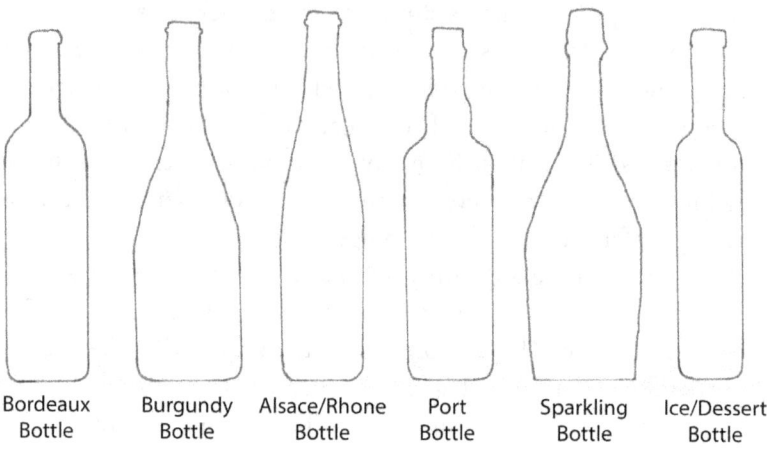

Image 8.2 An illustration showing the six basic shapes of wine bottles. Source: Illustration by the author.

The shapes are also pretty specific, relating to the amount of oxygen in the bottle and how the sediment can settle within the bottles. I have included a rough chart I made (see Image 8.2) to give you an idea of the general shape of the different categories of wine bottles. Here is a bit more information about each shape as well.

1. Bordeaux: the most traditional bottle shape. Originated in the Bordeaux region of France. It has straight sides and high distinctive shoulders. It is the most common wine bottle shape the world over. Most associated with Merlot, Malbec, and Cabernets.
2. Burgundy: created in the Burgundy region of France, this bottle has a wide base and graceful sloping shoulders leading to a short neck. This bottle was an easy shape for early glass blowers to make. Used extensively for Chardonnay and Pinot Noir.
3. Alsace/Rhone: this bottle tends to be thinner and more delicate then the first two shapes, similar in design to the Burgundy but with a longer neck. The shape originated in the Alsace region of France. It is most associated with Riesling wine.
4. Port: this bottle is very similar in shape to the Bordeaux bottle but it has a bulb in the neck which is designed to catch sediment, created from the ageing process, when this wine is poured.

5. Sparkling: these bottles tend to be thicker and heavier to protect them from exploding due to the pressure of the bubbles. They tend to have a deep punt (the indent on the bottom of the bottle) which also increases strength. Classic champagnes will be in darker bottles allowing for aging, while sparkling rose will often be in a clear bottle to allow the color of the wine to be displayed.
6. Ice/dessert: these bottles are generally tall and thin and hold roughly half the volume of the other wine bottles. This is because these wines tend to be sweeter so less is consumed.

82 SETTING THE PROPER TABLE

There are three generally accepted table settings, all of which have their uses in the prop world, depending on the show. The three types are Casual, informal/semi-formal, and Formal. Below are diagrams of each, along with written descriptions and some information to help understand them. Some general things to keep in mind: the diagrams below are examples of the idea of each of the types of settings; if you are doing a Formal meal set-up but are not serving oysters, then you would not set the Oyster fork – only set the silverware, glassware, etc. for the courses you are serving. Remember, the basic idea is to access the items (utensils and drinkware) you will be using in order as efficiently as possible so the guest(s) know what to use and when. The general rule of thumb is that utensils should be set from the outside in on each side of the plate in the order they will be used.

Casual /Basic Place setting: (see Image 8.3) Most often seen with the Napkin (6) to the left of the plate with the fork (5) resting on top of it, or the right of it. To the right of the plate is the knife (3), with the blade facing the plate and a spoon (if needed) to the outside (right) of the knife. The water glass/goblet (2) goes above the knife on the right side of the setting. The variation of this is that all three pieces of silverware can be placed on the left side of the plate, all on top of the napkin, with the fork closest to the plate, followed by the knife (blade facing the plate) and then the spoon to the outside (furthest left). Generally, in Casual settings, placemats (1) are used instead of, or in conjunction with, a tablecloth.

Informal/Semi-Formal setting: (see Image 8.4) This setting elevates a dining event and is used chiefly when a few courses will be served. It makes the meal feel special but not stuffy. This semi-formal setting often includes a bread plate (1) and butter knife (2) at each setting to the upper left of the plate with the knife handle

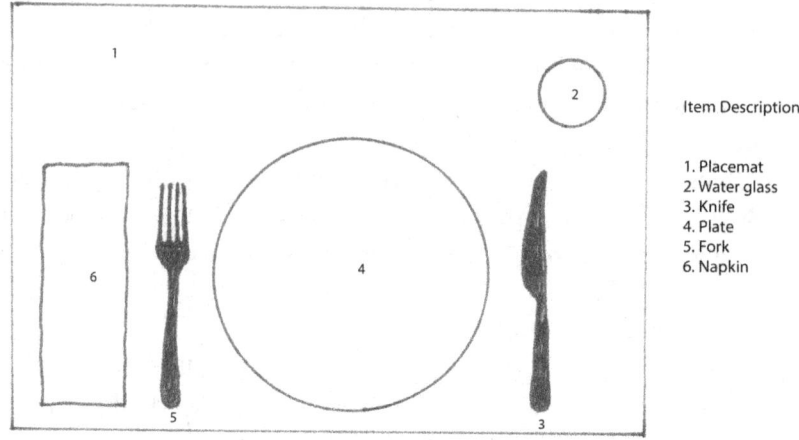

Image 8.3 An illustration of a casual place setting with elements numbered and listed out.

Source: Illustration by the author.

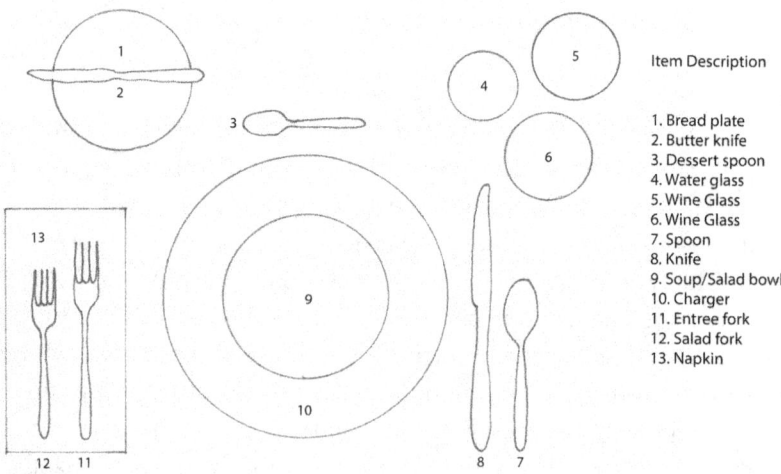

Image 8.4 An illustration of a semi-formal place setting with elements numbered and listed out.

Source: Illustration by the author.

on the right side and blade facing the guest. (all place settings are set with the understanding that most people are right-handed.) Dessert utensil(s) (3) centered above the charger (see more information about chargers in the next paragraph), at least one wine glass (5&6) to the far right top, and the water glass/goblet (4) to the inside of the wine glass(es). The Charger (10) is centered in front of each guest and can have the soup bowl (9) placed upon it as part of the table setting. Semi-Formal place settings can often have several additional utensils, depending on whether you serve an appetizer salad or soup. The minimum silverware should include an entree knife (8) to the right of the charger and closest to it with the blade facing in, with a soup spoon (7) to the right of the knife. An entrée fork should be closest to the charger on the left with a salad fork to the left of it. The forks can be placed on the napkin (as shown) or the napkin can be placed to the left of the forks, space may be the deciding force on that arrangement. Remember only to place the utensils that you need.

With the Semi-Formal and Formal settings, you often add a charger to the table set-up. This is a larger, more decorative plate upon which the individual courses are placed. Charger plates serve both aesthetic and practical purposes. They enhance and elevate the table décor while protecting the table and tablecloth from becoming dirty, they also help retain heat in the dinnerware. Some people suggest the charger be removed once the entrée is served, while others prefer and recommend that it stay for the entirety of the meal.

Another distinction between casual and other more formal settings is the idea that you should only touch each item when needed, so generally, in Semi-Formal and Formal settings, silverware is generally not placed on the napkin. In Semi-Formal the napkin is still set to the left of the forks on the left of the plate, or the forks are placed on it. In Formal settings, the napkin is often folded in a decorative style and placed upon the charger to give the table a more decorative and elegant atmosphere and also so guests must place it upon their laps or tuck it in at their collar before the first course is served.

Formal place setting – This setting is for the most formal/traditional of meals, black tie dinners, multi-course holiday feasts, and the like (see Image 8.5). More than the other two, this setting relies significantly on the exact items being served. If you are having a fish course, an additional fork and knife are added; if Oysters are served,

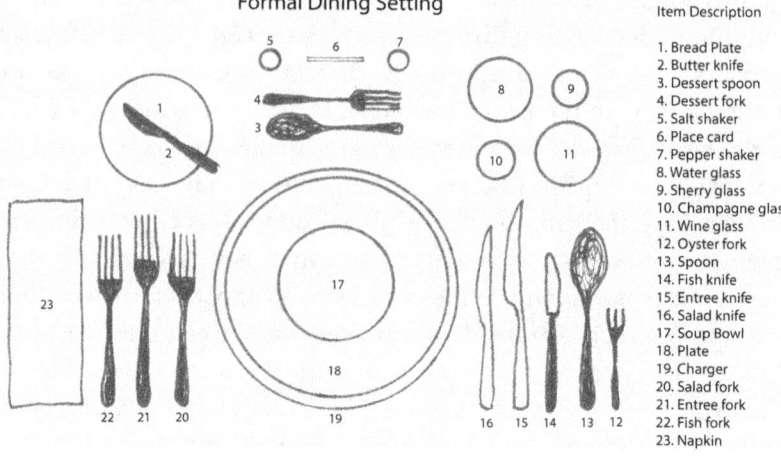

Image 8.5 An illustration of a formal place setting with elements numbered and listed out.

Source: Illustration by the author.

a special fork is added. A champagne flute may accompany the three other glasses on the table. Much of the setup is similar to the Semi-formal setting.

General layout of the Formal setting: Bread plate at the top left (1), with the butter knife (2) on top, knife handle facing to the right, and blade facing the guest. Dessert utensils are centered above the charger, with the dessert spoon (3) closer to the charger, and the cake fork (4) above. Water glass (8) is closer to the dessert utensils, with a sherry glass (9) to the right of it. A champagne flute (10) sits below the water glass/goblet with a wine glass (11) to the right of it. If champagne is not being served that glass can be switched out for a second wine glass, with the white wine glass slightly closer to the guest and below the water glass, with the red wine glass further away from the guest and to the right of the white wine glass. The Charger (19) should be centered, and depending on the host can have a dinner plate (18) and a soup bowl (17) placed upon it. The napkin (23) is generally folded and placed on the charger if the plate and bowl are not present, though it can also be placed to the left of the place setting as in the illustration. The appetizer fork (22) will be furthest left of the charger and then the entrée fork (21) in the middle, if a salad is to be served the salad form (20) goes closest to the charger. On the right of the charger, the salad knife (16) is placed closest to the charger (blade facing the charger), followed by the entree knife (15) (also blade in), then the appetizer knife (14), followed by the soup spoon (13), and finally the oyster fork (12) to the outside furthest right. All silverware should be spaced about ½" apart and with the bottom of the utensils, even with the bottom edge of the charger. If individual salt and pepper shakers (5 & 7) are used, they are placed above the dessert utensils and on either side of a place card holder (6), which should be centered above the overall setting.

83 NEWSPAPER FORMATS

There are many different newspaper formats with multiple variations within countries. Below are listed most of the more common sizes with measurements in both metric and imperial. These have changed over time, and while I could not find specific dates when major papers changed size, I have found over the years that older newspapers (pre-World War II) tended to be larger formats. The largest newspaper format is known as a broadsheet. It takes its name from a popular print type, a single-sided single sheet containing different kinds of material and content.

Format	Width × Height (mm)	Width × Height (in)
Vintage Broadsheet	597 × 749	23.5 × 29.5
US Broadsheet	381 × 578	15 × 22.8
British Broadsheet	375 × 597	14.8 × 23.5
South African Broadsheet	410 × 578	16.1 × 22.8
Ciner	350 × 500	13.8 × 19.7
Compact	280 × 430	11 × 16.9
Nordisch	400 × 570	15.7 × 22.4
Rhenish	350 × 520	13.8 × 20.5
Swiss	320 × 475	12.6 × 18.7
Tabloid	280 × 430	11 × 16.9
Canadian Tabloid	260 × 368	10.2 × 14.5
Norwegian Tabloid	280 × 400	11 × 15.7
New York Times	305 × 559	12 × 22
Wall Street Journal	305 × 578	12 × 22.8
Berliner	315 × 470	12.4 × 18.5

84 ENVELOPES SIZING

European (international) envelopes follow a system of sizes where the paper sizes and envelopes correspond to each other; American envelopes sadly do not do the same thing. The United States has three main types of envelopes: Commercial, Announcement, and Catalog. Within each of those types, there are various sizes. Here is a bit about each type, followed by a chart of the envelope format and its size in metric and Imperial measurements.

a. Commercial Envelopes. These are often called office envelopes and are used primarily in business settings, legal and financial mail, and professional correspondence. The most used commercial envelope is No. 10, which can fit a letter-sized piece of paper folded in thirds. You can fold a legal-sized piece of paper four times, fitting into a no. 10 envelope.

b. Announcement envelopes: These are often referred to as A series envelopes. They are mainly used for invitations, photographs, and greeting cards. They are squarer in shape (though still rectangular) than commercial envelopes, which tend to be longer, thinner rectangles. The most commonly used sizes of announcement envelopes are A2 and A9. These both are sometimes used for personal letter writing as the A9 can hold a letter-sized piece of paper folded in half, and an A2 can hold a letter-sized paper folded in quarters (once in each direction).

c. Catalog envelopes are most commonly used for catalogs (go figure), brochures, and other large-format mail that does not want to be folded. They are almost always made with a center seam to make them more durable. They have a similar size ratio to the announcement envelopes, being more square rectangular shapes.

Format	Width × Height (mm)	Width × Height (in)
6¼	152 × 89	6 × 3.5
6¾	165 × 92	6.5 × 3.6
7	172 × 95	6.8 × 3.7
7¾ Monarch	191 × 98	7.5 × 3.9
8⅝	219 × 92	8.6 × 3.6

(Continued)

Format	Width × Height (mm)	Width × Height (in)
9	225 × 98	8.9 × 3.9
10	241 × 104	9.5 × 4.1
11	264 × 114	10.4 × 4.5
12	279 × 121	11 × 4.8
14	292 × 127	11.5 × 5
16	305 × 152	12 × 6
A1	92 × 130	3.6 × 5.1
A2	146 × 111	5.7 × 4.4
A4	159 × 108	6.3 × 4.3
A6	165 × 121	6.5 × 4.8
A7	184 × 133	7.2 × 5.2
A8	206 × 140	8.1 × 5.5
A9	222 × 146	8.7 × 5.7
A10	241 × 152	9.5 × 6
A	225 × 98	8.9 × 3.9
1	229 × 152	9 × 6
1¾	241 × 152	9.5 × 6
3	254 × 178	10 × 7
6	267 × 191	10.5 × 7.5
8	286 × 210	11.3 × 8.3
9¾	286 × 222	11.3 × 8.7
10½	305 × 229	12 × 9
12½	318 × 241	12.5 × 9.5
13½	330 × 254	13 × 10
14½	368 × 292	14.5 × 11.5
15	381 × 254	15 × 10
15½	394 × 305	15.5 × 12

International (European) standard envelope sizes are defined by a series of international standards (ISO 269); these envelope sizes are generally related to paper sizes, which are defined by another international standard (ISO 216). The most common international envelope sizes are from the C series. The DL (Dimension lengthwise) envelope is the most common international business envelope. Similarly to the United States, an A4 sheet of paper (being closest in size to a United States letter-sized piece of paper) folded three times will fit into a DL envelope.

Format	Width × Height (mm)	Width × Height (in)
DL	110 × 220	4.3 × 8.7
B4	250 × 353	9.8 × 13.9
B5	176 × 250	6.9 × 9.8
B6	125 × 176	4.9 × 6.9
C3	324 × 458	12.8 × 18
C4	229 × 324	9 × 12.8
C4M	318 × 229	12.5 × 9
C5	162 × 229	6.4 × 9
C6/C5	114 × 229	4.5 × 9
C6	114 × 162	4.5 × 6.4
C64M	318 × 114	12.5 × 4.5
C7/C6	81 × 162	3.2 × 6.4
C7	81 × 114	3.2 × 4.5
CE4	229 × 310	9 × 12.2
CE64	114 × 310	4.5 × 12.2
E4	220 × 312	8.7 × 12.3
EC45	220 × 229	8.7 × 9
EC5	155 × 229	6.1 × 9
E5	115 × 220	4.5 × 8.7
E56	155 × 155	6.1 × 6.1
E6	110 × 155	4.3 × 6.1
E65	110 × 220	4.3 × 8.7
R7	120 × 135	4.7 × 5.3
S4	250 × 330	9.8 × 13
S5	185 × 255	7.3 × 10
S65	110 × 225	4.3 × 8.9
X5	105 × 216	4.1 × 8.5
EX5	155 × 216	6.1 × 8.5

85 AMERICAN PAPER SIZES

American paper sizes fall into roughly three categories, each with specific traits worth noting. The three categories are Loose sizes, ANSI, and Architectural. A bit of info on each of these followed by a breakdown of the formats and sizes in metric and imperial measurements.

Loose sizes: For a very long time in America, paper did not have consistent ratios, unlike the European ISO standards, which do. This makes scaling between paper sizes more difficult in the United States. The most common paper size in the United States is the Letter size paper (8.5" × 11").

ANSI: in 1996, the United States adopted standards set by the American National Standards Institute (ANSI). The standards adopted were ANSI Y14.1, which defines specific paper sizes based on the US letter size (8.5" × 11"), which also became known as ANSI A. If you double ANSI A, you get ANSI B, also known as Ledger or Tabloid, and that doubling in size continues up through ANSI E. Thus, all the ANSI sizes are proportional to each other but do not relate to different loose paper sizes established before the standard and very much in everyday use still today.

Architecture sizes: to make matters more complicated, architects prefer papers that have aspect ratios that are related to the ratios of small whole numbers like 4:3 and 3:2. So they have a different set of commonly used sizes that were also defined in 1996 by the same ANSI standard (y14.1). These papers are generally much larger and are for large format work (some of these are commonly used in theatrical drafting work by designers)

Format	Width × Height (mm)	Width × Height (in)
Letter	216 × 279	8.5 × 11
Legal	216 × 356	8.5 × 14
Tabloid	279 × 432	11 × 17
Ledger	432 × 279	17 × 11
Junior Legal	127 × 203	5 × 8
Half Letter	140 × 216	5.5 × 8.5
Government Letter	203 × 267	8 × 10.5
Government Legal	216 × 330	8.5 × 13
ANSI A	216 × 279	8.5 × 11
ANSI B	279 × 432	11 × 17
ANSI C	432 × 559	17 × 22
ANSI D	559 × 864	22 × 34
ANSI E	864 × 1118	34 × 44
Arch A	229 × 305	9 × 12
Arch B	305 × 457	12 × 18
Arch C	457 × 610	18 × 24
Arch D	610 × 914	24 × 36
Arch E	914 × 1219	36 × 48
Arch E1	762 × 1067	30 × 42
Arch E2	660 × 965	26 × 38
Arch E3	686 × 991	27 × 39

86 INTERNATIONAL PAPER SIZES

The most commonly used paper size category internationally is the A series. It is defined by the ISO 216 standard, though it was adopted in Europe in the 19th century and, except for the United States and Canada, is used throughout the rest of the world. A4 is the most common paper size, which is 210 mm × 297 mm (8.27 inches × 11.7 inches). This is slightly narrower and longer than the US letter-size paper. Unlike US papers, which are numbered from smallest to largest, the International paper generally follows a system of the larger papers having smaller numbers. Within the series, they are proportional, so cutting an A0 in half parallel to its smaller sides gets you two sheets of A1 (as an example). The A series papers use an aspect ratio of 1: the square root of 2. Since the square root often yields decimal places, the standard length and width are rounded to the nearest millimeter.

Format	Width × Height (mm)	Width × Height (in)
A0	841 × 1,189	33.1 × 46.8
A1	594 × 841	23.4 × 33.1
A2	420 × 594	16.5 × 23.4
A3	297 × 420	11.7 × 16.5
A4	210 × 297	8.3 × 11.7
A5	148 × 210	5.8 × 8.3
A6	105 × 148	4.1 × 5.8
A7	74 × 105	2.9 × 4.1
A8	52 × 74	2 × 2.9
A9	37 × 52	1.5 × 2
A10	26 × 37	1 × 1.5
A11	18 × 26	0.7 × 1
A12	13 × 18	0.5 × 0.7
A13	9 × 13	0.4 × 0.5
2A0	1,189 × 1,682	46.8 × 66.2
4A0	1,682 × 2,378	66.2 × 93.6
A0+	914 × 1,292	36 × 50.9
A1+	609 × 914	24 × 36
A3+	329 × 483	13 × 19

B series: The dimensions of the B series are also defined by the ISO 216 international paper standard. The B series is less common than the A series, created to give sizes not in the A series but between them. So, a B1 sheet is between an A0 and an A1 sheet in size. The B series also uses the aspect ratio of 1: square root of 2. The B series is used less commonly in offices but more for specialty situations like posters, books, and envelopes.

Format	Width × Height (mm)	Width × Height (in)
B0	1,000 × 1,414	39.4 × 55.7
B1	707 × 1,000	27.8 × 39.4
B2	500 × 707	19.7 × 27.8
B3	353 × 500	13.9 × 19.7
B4	250 × 353	9.8 × 13.9
B5	176 × 250	6.9 × 9.8
B6	125 × 176	4.9 × 6.9
B7	88 × 125	3.5 × 4.9
B8	62 × 88	2.4 × 3.5
B9	44 × 62	1.7 × 2.4
B10	31 × 44	1.2 × 1.7
B11	22 × 31	0.9 × 1.2
B12	15 × 22	0.6 × 0.9
B13	11 × 15	0.4 × 0.6
B0+	1,118 × 1,580	44 × 62.2
B1+	720 × 1,020	28.3 × 40.2
B2+	520 × 720	20.5 × 28.3

The C series: this size is defined by a different international standard than the A or B series. C is defined by the ISO 269 paper size standard. This size is most commonly used for envelopes. The C series paper size is the geometric mean of the areas of the A and B series papers of the same number. Meaning it falls between the A series and B series in size (slightly larger than A and marginally smaller than B). An A4 piece of paper will fit nicely into a C4 envelope. If folded in half, parallel to its smaller sides, it will fit into a C5 envelope; if folded in half again, it will fit into a C6 envelope (etc.). In my research, the C series is rare for printing or the like; the use of envelopes is relatively standard and well-established.

Format	Width × Height (mm)	Width × Height (in)
C0	917 × 1,297	36.1 × 51.1
C1	648 × 917	25.5 × 36.1
C2	458 × 648	18 × 25.5
C3	324 × 458	12.8 × 18
C4	229 × 324	9 × 12.8
C5	162 × 229	6.4 × 9
C6	114 × 162	4.5 × 6.4
C7	81 × 114	3.2 × 4.5
C8	57 × 81	2.2 × 3.2
C9	40 × 57	1.6 × 2.2
C10	28 × 40	1.1 × 1.6

87 BASIC PERIOD STYLES AND THEIR TIME PERIODS

Not all styles or time periods are covered here; that would be nearly impossible. Over my 30+ year career I have had to research all of the periods/styles listed below, each time I do I update the years associated with the style if I find they differ from what I have had in the past. The list is in chronological order based on the starting year of the style. Periods overlapped or moved across continents over a period of time, so shoulder areas exist as things transitioned from one era/period to another, so motifs or characteristics of one style will creep into another style. Influences vary widely and as communication became easier styles homogenized and transitioned faster. Do not use the list below as a hard and fast rule, but more as a springboard for research and learning as you dive into period productions. Unless making a specific statement about a period in a play it is common for pieces from multiple periods to exist in the same play depending on the nature of the piece. (See Tip 89 in Chapter Nine.)

Period/Style	Year Range (approx.)
Ancient Egyptian	3000–2000 BC
Ancient Greek/Roman	2000–300 BC
Medieval	500–1450
Renaissance	1350–1550

(Continued)

Period/Style	Year Range (approx.)
Elizabethan	1558–1603
Jacobean	1567–1649
Baroque	1643–1700
Louis XIV	1643–1715
Colonial	1650–1780
William and Mary	1689–1735
Queen Anne	1700–1755
Georgian	1714–1820
Regence	1715–1723
Pennsylvania Dutch	1720–1830
Louis XV	1723–1765
Rococo	1725–1775
Louis XVI	1750–1793
Chippendale	1750–1790
Neoclassic	1760–1789
Hepplewhite	1765–1800
Sheraton	1780–1820
Federal	1780–1820
Directoire	1789–1804
Revival	1800–1900
Empire	1805–1815
Regency	1811–1830
Restoration	1815–1830
Victorian	1837–1910
Arts and crafts	1880–1910
Art Nouveau	1880–1914
Edwardian	1890–1910
Art Deco	1920–1945
Bauhaus	1919–1933
Modern	1930–1945
Scandinavian contemporary	1930–1950
Contemporary	1980–present

Prop knowledge

Nine

There are so many tips and tricks that some don't fit a specific category; they are more "general," and this chapter is a collection of some of those things. Many of these are things you learn over time and vastly improve the product you put into the productions you work on. Some of them should be taught in every theater program available, though few are. I hope you find at least one item in this chapter to be an "aha" moment that will stick with you as you advance in your career.

88 WHAT IS "PERIOD"?

The word "Period" has a lot of definitions, but for our context, I am going to use three taken from Merriam-Webster: the first two nouns, the third an adjective:

1. (Noun) a chronological division, a division of geological time longer than an epoch and included in an era.
2. (Noun) a stage of culture having a definable place in time and space.
3. (Adjective) of, relating to, or representing a particular historical period.

We should focus mainly on the second and third definitions. Everything is of a period, even modern-day and postmodern. Do not accept the designer or director saying they need something to be "period." Make sure the items are appropriate for the setting and the time period. Sometimes, you can ask the dramaturg for help determining period-appropriate information, but often, you should do the research yourself; you will know it is correct, and you will gain the knowledge for future use.

When working on "period" pieces (Shakespeare, etc.), directors and designers often choose to set the play in a different period than it was initially written to be performed in. Try to ascertain from them why that choice is being made; it will help inform the decisions you and the designer make about the props and dressing to ensure that you are helping to support the period shift. Again, researching and making smart choices will help the audience understand the context of the play in this different period setting.

All that being said, sometimes (often) directors will ask for props, costumes, or other things that are anachronistic to the period in which the play is being set; you should ask about these choices to understand why they want them but know that ultimately sometimes they don't have a good reason they just want the thing. You can do the research and know the facts and then work with the designer to create the most realistically appropriate period item to fulfill the desire of the director. We recently did a production of The Tempest, for which the director stated he wanted the show to be "timeless." While that may sound easy, it was quite a challenge. We had several meetings where we discussed in detail what we would use to represent the specific props mentioned in the text. They mention flasks, mugs, casks, etc. Figuring out what these items would be so that the story was still clear to the audience proved to be a daunting task.

In another example, several years ago, we produced Les Mis, and the actors needed rifles for the barricade scene. Our budget was tight, and our runs were long, so renting "period-appropriate" blank-firing rifles was beyond our means. We bought some blank-firing rifles from our gun supplier and dressed them up as best we could to look like the period-appropriate rifles we wanted for the scene while still allowing them to fire and be cleaned appropriately. Throughout our 12-week run, we got at least three letters from patrons explaining that the guns we used onstage were not period-accurate. I took the time to email each of those patrons and explain our predicament of time, budget, and length of run and that we made the best choice we could within the circumstances. They responded and said they understood but wanted us to know they had noticed.

89 NOT EVERYTHING IS NEW, AND NOT EVERYONE IS WELL-TO-DO

It is essential to understand when a play is set and what that means for furniture and dressing. At the beginning of most scripts, a description of the setting and a time period are often listed. Don't allow yourself or the designer to fall into the trap of researching that exact date or period. This is one of my biggest pet peeves (I have probably said that 15 times in this book). Understand the context of the story and the characters. What is the location's story, how long have the characters lived there, do they have hand-me-downs from previous generations(s), and what helps to tell the story and convey the piece's meaning? Also, think about the characters in the story and their socio-economic status within the context of the play. Scrooge's apartment dressing should be vastly different than anything you would pull for the Cratchits.

In a recent production of *A Raisin in the Sun*, our designer was very aware of this and ensured that nearly everything we pulled for furniture and set dressing was from 20 to 40 years earlier than the play's setting (mid-1950s). This allowed the audience to believe and understand that this family had lived in this apartment for a long time, and they kept repairing and reusing the items and did not spend money on buying new things. When contemporary items were introduced into the play (the gifts given to Beneatha, etc.), their more modern and clean look helped to reinforce the idea that the things in the apartment had been there for a long time.

90 WAYS TO HELP THE PERFORMER TELL THE STORY

We work with the actors to ensure the props we provide allow them to make their performance believable. How realistic can we make the props without breaking the time or money bank? We research appropriate papers, types of writing or printing, location specifics like zip codes or phone numbers, and as much authentic information as we can create and deliver to immerse the actors in reality so they can focus on creating a believable performance for the audience. Sometimes, it is a lot of extra work, and no one in the audience can see the details that we put into the props, but the actors can, and that is worth it if it helps them deliver a better performance.

Two specific examples spring to mind. We work with many returning actors year after year, and early in my time at the Shakespeare Festival, I was doing some paper props for a messenger character in a history play. I spent the time copying out the text from the script for the documents this character was to deliver. I sent the documents to rehearsal, and that afternoon, the actor playing the messenger popped into the shop. He explained to me that he had dyslexia and worked really hard to memorize his lines, and if he looked down at the document and saw a word he recognized, it would throw him off, and he would probably lose the lines in his head. He asked if I could translate the documents into Italian or French so that if he looked down at them, he wouldn't recognize any word, which would help him with his performance. I did it, and for every show he returned for (six years' worth), we would translate his documents to help him and his performance.

In another instance, we were doing *Room Service,* and one of the characters had to go through a pile of bills and read them to the other characters. The director wanted a large stack of bills, but the character only reads off six of them. The actor wanted it to look like he was pulling them out of the pile randomly, but he wanted to pull out the correct bills each time. It took a little brainstorming, but we found a solution that worked for everyone. The bills the actor needed to pull out were all printed on different tones of yellow paper, while the rest were on other colors or white paper. We went so far as to use the lightest yellow for the first bill mentioned and went through to the darkest yellow for the last bill mentioned so that he could look and shuffle through them and still pull out the correct bill in the proper order every time.

91 BASIC KNOTS EVERYONE SHOULD KNOW

Here are five knots used regularly in props and life in general. You should learn these knots and be able to tie them whenever the need arises. There are many other valuable knots, but knowing these five will make your life easier, generally speaking, and they are effective in many instances where a knot is required.

A few terms that will help with the explanations below. Live end: this is the end of the rope you actively use to tie the knot. It is the loose end that can move about (live). Dead-end: this is the end of the rope away from where you are tying the knot; in many knots, it is the rope that is secured to an object that you are then using the live end to tie to create the knot. Breaking the knot: a way to loosen the ropes so the knot becomes easier to untie.

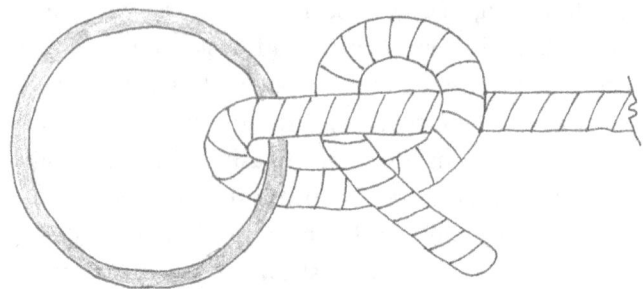

Image 9.1 An illustration showing the steps to tie a half hitch.
Source: Illustration by the author.

Half hitch

The half hitch is one of the simplest knots to tie. You probably do this in your life quite often and don't even realize it. It is the knot used to secure the end of a rope, add a locking knot to a clove hitch or a truckers hitch, and add a lump of thread on the end of a sewing string so it doesn't pull through the fabric.

Tying the knot: (See Image 9.1 for a visual reference of the steps as described here.)

Take the live end of the rope and make a loop. Pass the live end through the loop from the rear side, adjust where on the string or rope you want the knot to be when it is tightened, and then pull both ends to tighten and secure the half hitch.

Clove hitch

The clove hitch is used to secure a rope to an object (a pipe, a board, or a similar object.) If tied correctly, it chinches up well and will remain secure under tension; if tension is released, the clove hitch can work itself loose. A way to avoid this is to end the knot with a half hitch until you break the knot. One nice thing about the clove hitch is that you can swivel/twist the knot around the object you're securing the rope, too; this allows exact placement of the knot and a way to tighten it to the object in question.

Tying the knot: (See Image 9.2 for a visual reference of the steps as described here.)

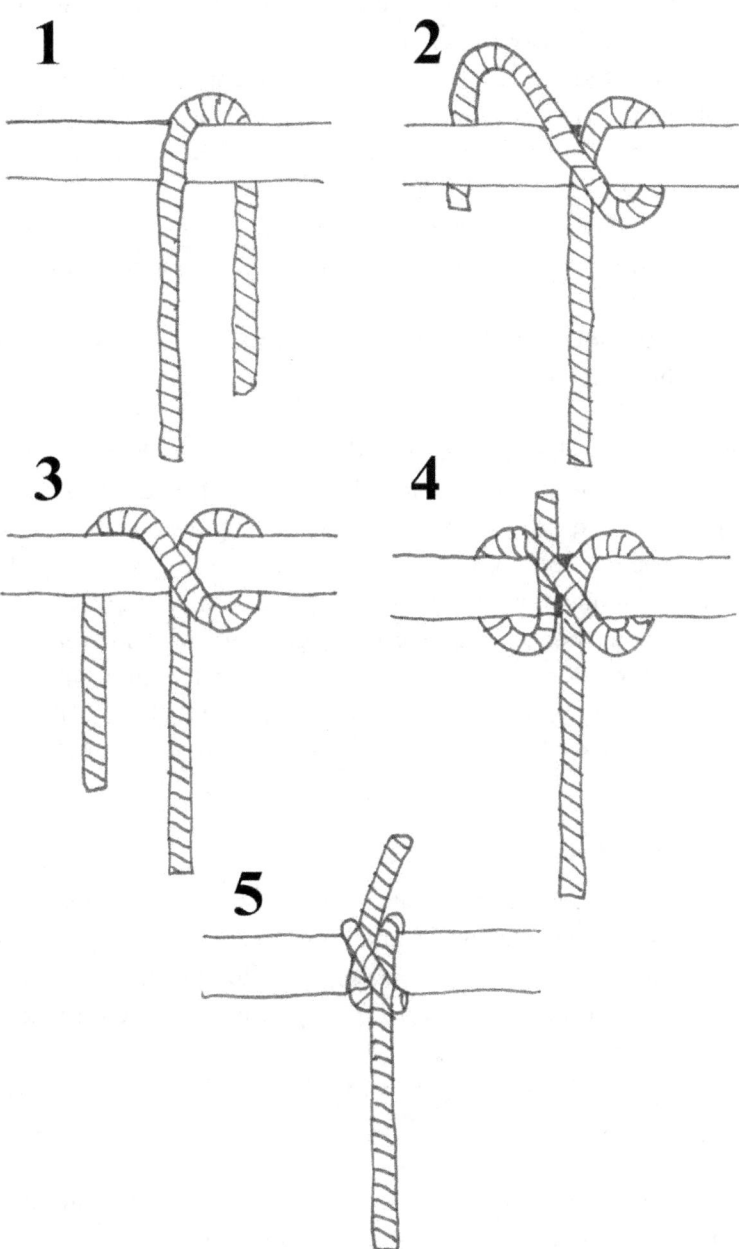

Image 9.2 Illustrations showing the steps to tie a clove hitch.
Source: Illustrations by the author.

1. Take the dead end of the rope let it drape over the thing you are about to tie the clove hitch to.
2. With the other hand, take the live end, wrap it under the object, and pull up and run the end around the left side of the dead end.
3. Once there, feed the live end back over the object you are tying to and bring it up to the left of the first wrap.
4. As you pull it up in front of the object, slide the live end under the first loop (between the dead end and the first loop to be exact, this will form an x.
5. Then pull down on the dead end while pulling up on the live end to tighten the knot.

You can slide all the ropes together (next to each other) before tightening to clean up the knot's look and help it cinch up tighter. Suppose the live or dead end needs to be lengthened, and you have enough rope to do it. In that case, you can work the excess rope from either side of the knot by rolling the knot around your object, feeding the rope from the too-long end to the shorter end, and working the live and dead ends back and forth, maintaining the knot but moving the excess rope. As mentioned earlier, finishing this knot with one or two half hitches will help secure it and not allow it to walk itself and loosen up.

Bowline

The bowline is a knot that creates a fixed loop at the rope's end that can be used to wrap around something. Once tied, this rope is relatively secure and tends not to loosen up. Flipping the knot over the can break it and make it reasonably easy to untie. More on that once we get it tied.

Tying the knot: (See Image 9.3 for a visual reference of the steps as described here.)

1. Take the live end of the rope and make a loop by draping the live end over the dead end of the rope. The live end should be on top of the dead end, forming a number "6" with a decent length tail.
2. Then, make a circle of rope to wrap around your object; it can be any size. Ensure you have enough rope on the live end to make the circle the size you need.

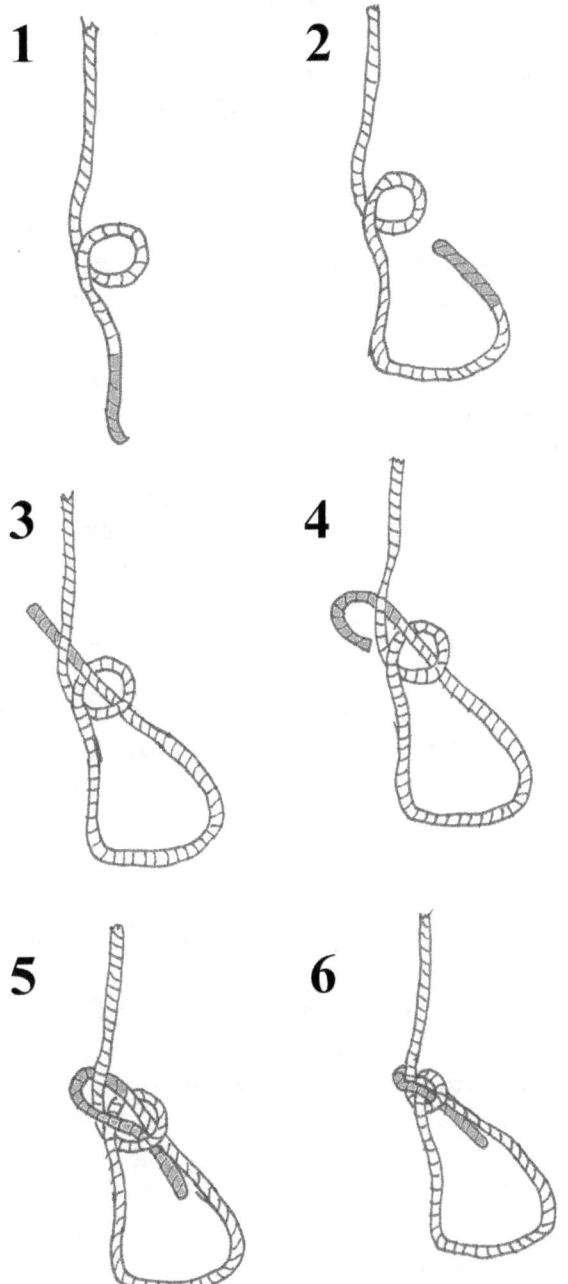

Image 9.3 Illustrations showing the steps to tie a bowline.
Source: Illustrations by the author.

3. Close the object holding circle, by running the live end up through the small loop (the six) you created when starting the knot.
4. Once through the six loop, you are going to go around the right side of the dead end of the rope and then push the live end forward around the left side of the dead end.
5. Once back in front, you are going to take the live end and put it back into the small loop.
6. Hold the live end and the large object holding loop in one hand and the dead end in the other and pull away from each other, tightening the knot until it is secure.

Now you have a tied loop that will not move around or change size on you. Another way to think of tying this knot is the tree, the hole, and the rabbit. So, to begin, you make a hole at the base of the tree (the tree being the dead end), ensuring the end of the hole wraps over the tree. Then, the rabbit (the live end) comes up through the hole, goes around the tree, and then back into the hole.

To break (loosen) the knot, you flip the rope over so you are looking at the back of the knot. Lift the knot so the dead end is lower than the knot; take the rope that is looped around the dead end and push it down toward the floor and away from the knot; this should pull the live end up and loosen the center of the knot making it easy to untie.

Trucker's hitch

The trucker's hitch is used to secure or strap down a load into a truck or onto a surface.

Tying the knot: (See Image 9.4 for a visual reference of the steps as described here.)

Secure one end of your rope onto your load or whatever you're tying down with a bowline knot. Make a slip knot toward the middle of your rope.

1. Start by making a loop in the rope. Then, fold a piece of the rope that's on top of the loop in on itself to make a bight.
2. Push the bight up through the loop and pull the slip knot tight.
3. Wrap the free end of the rope around a post, tree, or whatever you use to anchor your load.

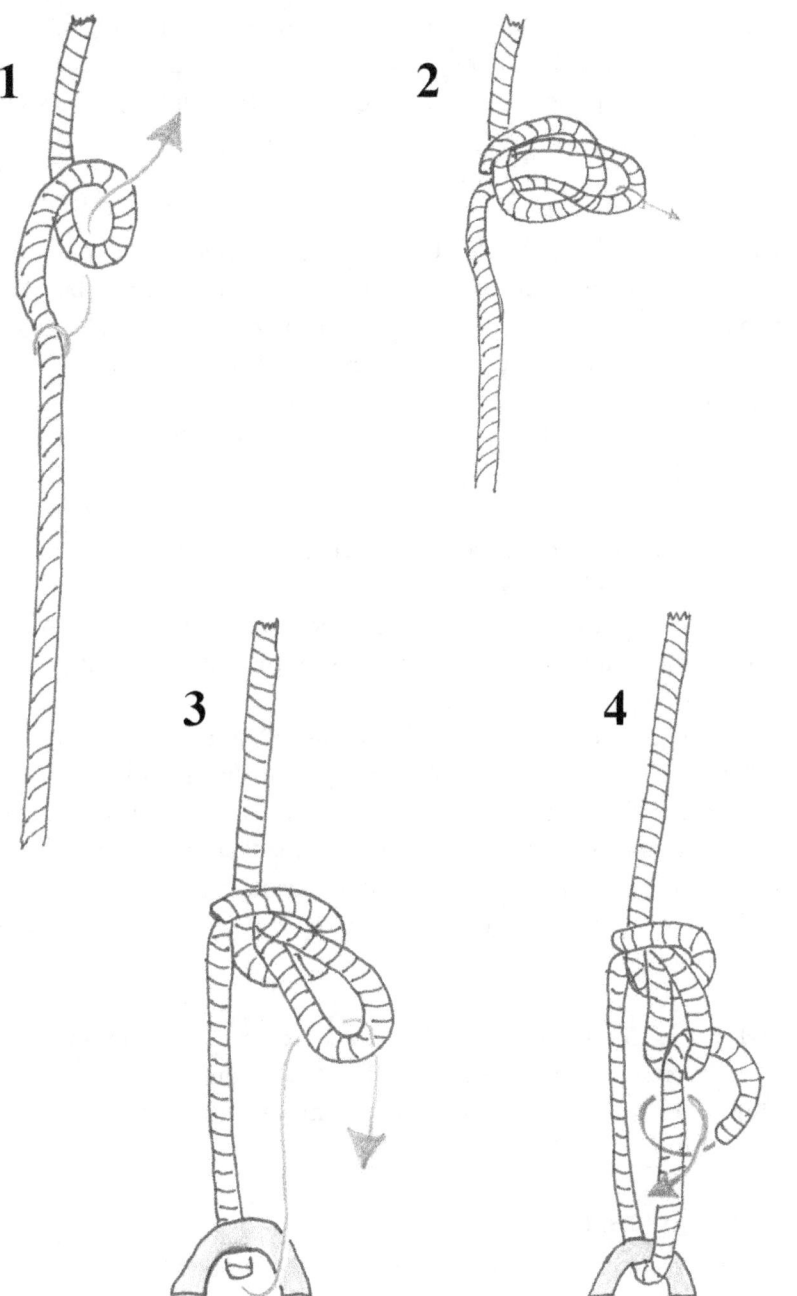

Image 9.4 Illustrations showing the steps to tie a truckers hitch.
Source: Illustrations by the author.

4. Feed the free end through the slip knot and pull it taught. Tie off the line by crossing under the taught rope below the slip knot, then wrap it under and back up through the slack. Pull it tight to secure the knot.

Square knot

The square knot is most useful when tying two pieces of rope together to make a longer piece of rope. The ropes do not need to be of the same diameter, but you will find it easier to tie if they are close in size; even with very differently sized ropes, it will work to secure the two together.

Tying the knot: (See Image 9.5 for a visual reference of the steps as described here.)

1. Hold one piece of rope in each hand, take the rope (striped) in your left hand and put it over the top of the rope (non-striped) in your right hand, then twist the striped rope under the non-striped rope and pull the ends of both ropes up toward you slightly.
2. Continuing with the striped rope push it to the left behind the non-striped rope, which is now on the left side.
3. Take the end of the non-striped rope and flip it over the striped rope and through the hole in the middle and pull it to the right. You should have created two loops of rope that are wrapped around each other as shown in step 3 of the illustration.
4. You then grab all four ends and pull away from the middle, tightening the knot.

Verbal way to remember this knot is Left over right and under, then right over left and under. Or as the Girl Scouts taught my wife: Right over left, then left over right, makes a square knot tighter than tight.

92 DATE THINGS

This may seem simple and not worth putting in this book, and it was hard to figure out where to place it, but it is so helpful in many ways in the prop world. I will give you a handful of examples below, but I would be liberal with dating things, as it never hurts to know when something arrives in your possession.

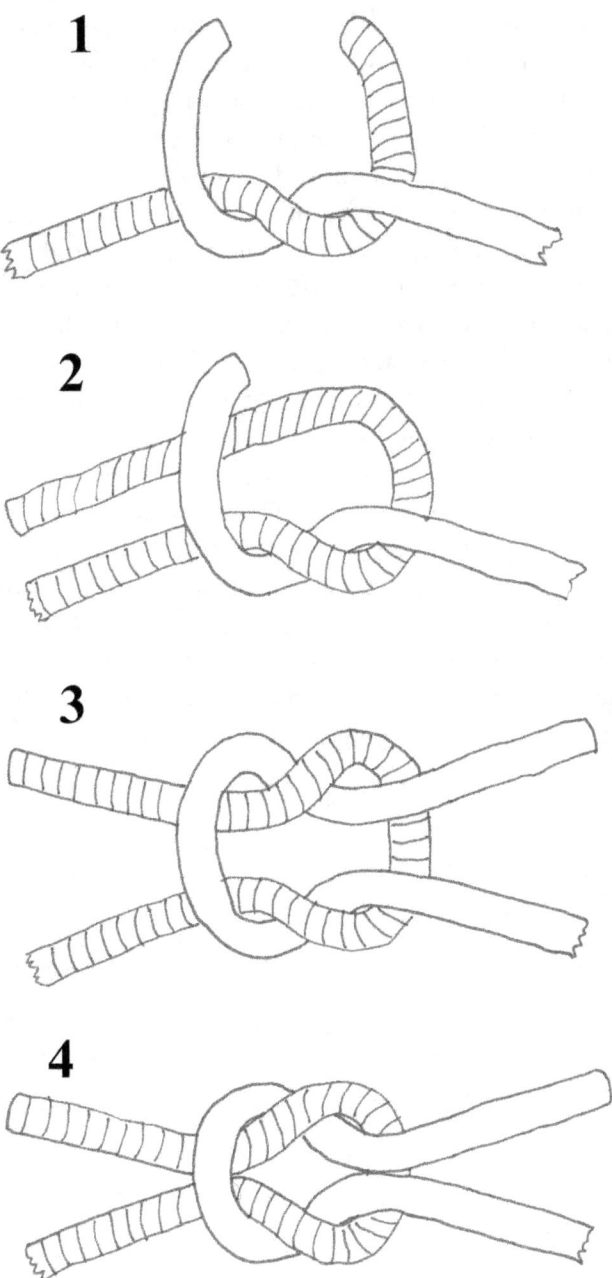

Image 9.5 Illustrations showing the steps to tie a square knot.
Source: Illustrations by the author.

Date any notes you take or revisions you make to things (particularly prop lists!). It is the worst to be working off outdated paperwork. I have gotten into the habit of whenever I open a document or a list, I save a new copy with the current date and then work on that document, so I have a record of the original or previous version. This way, any updates are reflected in the most up-to-date copy.

Put dates on tools when they are first introduced in the shop. This way, you know how old a tool is, so you will know when it might be nearing the end of its life span. We also date when we buy batteries for our cordless devices. Particularly recently, we have been buying off-brand batteries to save money, and we can see if the non-branded batteries hold up as well as the branded ones. We also can use the dates on tools to plan for routine maintenance.

Put dates on liquid materials in the shop (paints, sealers, glues, etc.). This will help you in several ways. It will let you and your staff know which items are oldest so they get used up first. Also, it will let you know how long something lasts, so you know how often you would need to replenish it. Two examples: our gold leaf size has lasted for seven years (gallon size), while our wood glue (also gallon size) lasts about four to six months. Finally, it will help you decide whether the item should be kept or if it has outlasted its usefulness.

Prop perspectives

Ten

Here are some thoughts that keep the job in perspective and remind you that it is not rocket science, and we are not curing cancer. That being said, we are doing important work. The ability for people to come to the theater or other places where live art is performed creates a special bond that is hard to describe. No two performances are exactly the same, so as an audience member, you are getting to witness in real time a piece of art being created; you and the other audience members seeing it together will be the only people ever to see that particular performance, which makes it really special. There is no editing, no redo's, it is happening, and you are along for the ride.

93   BE FEARLESS

Try things, experiment, and learn as much from your successes as your failures. You will fall down, you will make mistakes, and that is ok. We often learn the most from those moments. It can be embarrassing or sad, but don't let it defeat you. Brush yourself off and move forward; knowing what won't work makes it easier to find what will. I think it was Thomas Edison who said (I am paraphrasing here), "I didn't fail to make the lightbulb work 1,000 times; I found 1,000 things that didn't work."

I have had multiple failures in my career; one that stands out to this day was for the Utah Shakespeare Festival's production of *Mary Poppins*. For the letter scene (in which Supercal … is sung), the designer designed a wagon on which two characters are to arrive onstage. During the song, they wanted the cart to expand in length from its original 7 feet to about 18 feet, and as it expanded, they wanted the word Supercalifragilisticexpialidocious to appear on the side of the wagon. I thought we could make this work, but physics got the better of us multiple times. We could not get the cart to maintain its shape and not collapse as it expanded. We were into tech, and it still wasn't working. Notes were piling up for dozens of other props in the show, so I finally had to admit defeat. I told the director and designer we could keep working on the cart and would probably figure it out (but I didn't promise anything). However, this would take all the time we had left, or I could direct my team to focus on the notes for all the other props in the show, and we could devise a different solution for the wagon. They agreed that completing all the other notes was important, so they gave up on the expanding cart. We created a pull-out banner with the word on it and made the wagon structural at the seven-foot size. Ultimately, it did not hurt the show (the audience never knew the cart had been designed to expand). We still found a fun and creative way to get the word displayed onstage, and the rest of the props got some attention, so the overall show was of a higher quality. To this day, however, I know that the cart didn't work how it was supposed to, and I sometimes dream about it and wake up thinking I have a solution.

This same thing comes up with my staff a lot in the shop: they feel they have "failed" and that it is a direct reflection on them if the project isn't right or perfect the first time. This, in my opinion, is one of the most significant issues facing creativity in the world today. You have to try things and learn what does and doesn't work. There are often multiple solutions to a problem, many of which might work in any given circumstance. The ability to give yourself permission to fail or to be wrong is sadly lacking today. Please don't beat yourself up because it didn't work; accept that you learned one way not to do it in the future, and plow ahead with another option.

94 EVERYONE IS AN ARTIST

I will repeat this – everyone is an artist. Everyone is creative; you need to find out in what way(s) your creativity manifests itself. I am a fan of Robert Fulghum, who wrote *All I Ever Really Needed to Know I Learned in Kindergarten*, along with many other books. I don't remember which book it is in, but he reflects on his years teaching and mentions that as children, we are all asked to draw things in school, to color, or to create, and in general, we all do and don't question whether we are good at it or not, we do it. Over time, others critique this creativity, and we begin to feel that we are not as good as others, that they are more "artistic," more "creative," and we don't have that "Artistic Gene" or that "creative bone." I call bull crap. We all are creative, some in different ways than others, but the innate ability to assemble, create, and express our emotions or feelings is in each of us.

Shut off the terrible critic in your head and allow yourself the permission to try things too, have fun, and express yourself in whatever way or with whatever medium you are comfortable with. Once you find something you feel comfortable with, keep doing it (don't think of it as practice – but in a way, it is). As you continue to do it, you will get better at it. Once you are comfortable with one creative outlet, give yourself a pat on the back and then find something else you want to try and do that too. Build your toolbox of creativity. Pull out the tools and use them regularly. Over time, you will find that your creativity is empowering and will motivate you to continue being creative. Don't be afraid – be a kid again and draw, paint, sing, and dance with abandon as if no one is watching, or if they are watching, you don't care, and you wish they would join you in being creative.

95 BE KIND TO EVERYONE

You never know when someone you have worked with may be able to recommend you or hire you in the future (don't burn bridges). This is a no-brainer and should be taught in all Intro to Theater classes. The theater world is very small and getting smaller; everyone knows everyone, and we talk to each other. Nearly every interview I have gotten was because I knew someone who worked at the theater or a close acquaintance. I landed my first year in Utah when I was a sophomore in college because my design professor and advisor was designing shows in one of the theaters at the Utah Shakespeare Festival. He recommended I apply to be on run-crew to get out, meet some people, and do some theater not in the Midwest. That first summer, I met amazing people who are still friends, and we still rely on each other to help solve problems or find employees for our respective organizations. That network has continued to grow and expand as I have moved into management and now hire staff each year who have gone on to impressive careers. We reach out to each other to find qualified people who we know will do an excellent job for us or the people we know. Many people who have worked for me early in their careers, while still in school or just having graduated, have moved on to their own careers and now manage prop departments at large theaters across the country or are lead artisans in shops. Connection and fellowship are essential and provide the networking needed to survive and thrive in this business. Often, the people you take a chance on become those who surprise you in their career paths and remain the closest connections you have moving forward. Seeing the potential in someone and encouraging that is always worth the time and effort.

96 INCLUDING YOURSELF

The job of props can be amazing and fulfilling, but at times it can be a drag; there are deadlines, budgets, and 15 different people telling you how it needs to be done, changed, or made better. Remember to take care of yourself, take breaks, and get out of your head. Take a step away from a project and remember that at the end of the day we are telling stories, not performing brain surgery. You, as a prop person, are contributing to the bigger picture, but you can't do that at 100% if you are sick or stressed out. Find ways to keep things in perspective. Be aware of your shortcomings and ask for help. Learn when you need a break and take it. Find the moments of joy in your work and elevate them. Know when you have worked enough hours in a day and go home, the work will still be there the next day, and with some sleep and the perspective of a new day, it might not seem as daunting. Learn to say "no" when it is appropriate, being the "yes" person can feel great in the moment, but if you are just piling on to your stress it is probably not worth it. You are great at what you do, but if you are not taking care of yourself, it will be hard to maintain that excellence. As a good friend says to me quite often when we are in the thick of it: "Just Breathe."

97 NEVER BE AFRAID TO ASK QUESTIONS

Never be afraid to ask questions or admit you don't know something. Early in my career, I was interviewing for a job and was asked if I knew how to use a lathe. I said yes, though I had never actually used one. I knew the theory of it and felt I could probably figure it out if it ever actually came up, which I assumed it wouldn't, and I really, really wanted the job. After two interviews, I got the job. I arrived a few weeks later to begin work, and the first project I was assigned was a table with four turned legs. The prop supervisor said the designer had drawn up the legs and did not want to purchase premade legs, so

I would need to turn them. Internally, I freaked out. I knew I was in a pickle because I told my bosses I had this skill. So, knowing I had put myself in a corner, I decided to figure it out. I went to the library and checked out two books on turning and lathe operation (the internet was new then, and YouTube, where there are now thousands of turning videos, did not exist). I poured over those books each evening, and each day, I went in and worked on the lathe, gaining confidence in the tools and the knowledge I was digesting each night. Within a short time, I learned the necessary skills to turn the legs and complete the table successfully.

There are better ways to do this. I do not recommend this approach ever. It was very stressful to be thrown a project that I said I could do but immediately knew I was not qualified for, and besides that, lying is never the answer. I learned several valuable lessons from that project. If I don't know how to do something, I tell people. Then, I take the time to try to learn that skill. Being honest upfront is always the best course of action, and it will build a relationship with those people that is invaluable in the long term. Then, take the fact that you know there is a new skill you can add to your toolbox and learn it. It will make you a better artisan/crafter moving forward, and you will gain confidence in your creative abilities. There are many ways to learn those new skills, which I will cover in the next Tip.

98 YOU ARE ALWAYS YOUNG ENOUGH TO LEARN A NEW SKILL

A few years back, we needed a breakaway vase for a production of *Murder for Two*. I did not know how to make greenware, as the few times I had needed it in the past, I had purchased it from a local ceramic shop. As we went into this production process, we learned our local ceramic shop had gone out of business. We are in a fairly remote area and did not think shopping for these items would be the best course of action. We determined that we should figure out how to make these items ourselves (adding a tool (skill) to our toolbox). So, I searched on YouTube and found multiple videos about slip casting and greenware; I picked three or four that seemed to show the process and spent 40 minutes watching them. We then bought a mold and some ceramic slip and gave it a shot. It took a little experimentation to figure out the timing of the steps to achieve the desired results, but the process went smoothly after that. We now make our own greenware on a fairly regular basis. There are many ways to learn new skills, from watching online videos and DIY instructions on websites to subscribing to things like Make magazine. Props is the perfect job for this type of lifelong learning; any new craft or artistic skill will be useful over your career.

As I write this, it is November of 2023, and a generous donor just gifted the prop shop at the Utah Shakespeare Festival a laser engraver/cutter and a 3D printer. The scene shop also installed a new CNC machine. We are slowly learning the software for all three machines and figuring out ways they can be useful to us in the props department. I am nearly 50, and the technology can sometimes make me feel much older, but breaking down the process and figuring things out one step at a time, finding practical applications for the technology, and slowly working on building up your confidence makes learning any new skill or tool worthwhile in the long run. In props creation, there are always new challenges, crazy ideas from designers, and new plays that require different ways of thinking about props and how we can achieve the goals set out by the design. I feel like I will never stop learning, and I don't want to; one of the true joys of this career is the ability to learn, play, and explore every day.

99   REMEMBER, YOU ARE NOT ALONE

Sometimes, when you are working on a project by yourself, and it is behind and tech week is looming, you can feel like there is no one to help you or that you are in this fight alone. That is far from the truth. There are thousands, if not tens of thousands, of prop people in many different careers and fields (television, movies, themed entertainment, theatrical production, window displays, cosplay, etc.) working on the same issues and dealing with the same problems that you are. Reach out and find them. There are Facebook groups, people on Instagram, videos on YouTube and TikTok, professional organizations, industry conferences, etc. Take a few minutes and do some searching, and you will find kindred spirits slogging through similar circumstances. They are out there and available to offer advice, help, and, most of all, support. This has been true in my career; when I started in the prop field, I was in the Midwest, and there were many theaters within driving distance to borrow things from and collaborate with on projects. I felt very alone when I moved to Utah and started working at the Shakespeare Festival. There are only one or two other major theaters in the state and only a few in the states surrounding us; I felt very isolated and unsure of myself. I contacted other professional prop people through the Society of Prop Managers. I found many people willing to offer advice, listen to issues, let me borrow/rent unique one-off props so I wouldn't need to build and store them knowing they wouldn't get used again, and mainly to support me with encouragement and words of advice.

100 RESEARCH AND PERIOD CORRECTNESS

Research and period correctness are important, but don't let them get in the way of good, clear storytelling. Knowing what is correct for the period and the action in a scene is great, but dying on that hill when it doesn't serve the production is not good for anyone involved. For many years at the Utah Shakespeare Festival, we had a producer who would question the authenticity of the props, asking if a ballpoint pen was period-appropriate for a scene or if the document on stage had writing on it, and if it was typed or handwritten. While it can sometimes be a bit demoralizing to deal with those types of questions, it also allowed me to learn a lot and be prepared for the questions. For each show, I would research the items I felt he would take issue with and would be prepared. When the notes came up, I was ready with dates, facts, and examples to show that we had done the research and were being period-appropriate with whatever prop or style thing was in question.

That being said, sometimes you need to know the information, share the information, and then allow the reality of the situation to take over and deal with the problem/issue at hand in the most appropriate way possible. In a recent season, we were doing a show set in 1957, and the scene called for someone to go out for coffee and bring back multiple to-go cups of the liquid. The director didn't want to deal with actual liquid, so they asked for lids for the cups. My assistant researched and found out that the to-go cup lid wasn't invented until about five years after the year in which the play was set. We shared that information with the director and also told her that we had ordered and would deliver as soon as they arrived, the most period-looking lid we were able to find for the cups we were using. The audience was none the wiser, and the lids solved a problem for the show. It did not damage or affect the storytelling negatively and helped the actors not to worry about spilling coffee on the set, costumes, themselves, or others.

This can be a fine line, and sometimes we lose the battles with the directors or designers and have to put something very period-inappropriate onstage for a production. If they feel strongly about it and they feel it helps to tell the story they are trying to tell, you should go along with it. I have the research and am prepared with it when a patron asks so they know that we are aware of the anachronistic situation but that we were doing as the creative vision behind the production asked us. We built a bike (modified a "modern" bike) for a production of William Shakespeare's *As You Like It* set in 1599, knowing full well that bikes weren't invented until several hundred years later. The designer had found a sketch by Leonardo Da Vinci of a wheeled personal device (looked like the idea most people would have of a bike), but like many of his thoughts and sketches, it was never realized during his lifetime. We used that image and a bicycle from our stock to create this vehicle for the production. I got more comments from patrons/guests about that bike than any other prop in my 30 years at the Festival. I shared the research and explained that the director really felt it would add to the silliness of the scene and provide a great moment of comic relief for the audience. We ignored the reality of the period and created our best representation of what would have been period appropriate to the best of our knowledge.

101 WE ARE ALL STORYTELLERS AT HEART

It is in the human DNA to share our story with those around us. This job allows us to elevate that level of storytelling and share not only our stories but the stories of the playwrights, directors, designers, actors, etc., through the use of objects. Thinking about the story when choosing props, particularly dressing can be really important to establishing clear storytelling. What things have the characters collected and kept throughout their lives, what is the significance of those items, and how do the objects help inform the audience about the characters both within the framework of the story we are telling now and in the backstory of the characters? Not every prop is a hero prop; very few are, but every prop should help tell the story, even if it is very subtle.

The ultimate goal is to help tell the story to the audience clearly. To do that well, you need to know the story in detail, understand the underlying message(s) that the director wants to impart with that particular production or scene, and then work with the designer(s) and the team of artists to make sure that all the props and dressing are propelling that message and story to the audience.

Never let your ego, the desire to be correct, or your knowledge of what is appropriate get in the way of making sure you are using all your ability and talent to contribute to the clearest possible storytelling in every production you do. Often, this goes unnoticed by the audience, but if it weren't done well, they would feel something was off. In a recent production of the musical *Jane Austen's Emma*, the designer wanted to tie the pieces of furniture together subtly so they would help inform the audience (subconsciously) about whose house we were in during any given scene. All the furniture for Hartfield (Emma's family's home) was upholstered in shades of turquoise blue, while all the furniture used in the Bates home was upholstered in brown fabrics. This is a subtle thing, but when I pointed it out to audience members, they all had a realization moment. This choice made during the design process helped clarify the storytelling for them in a way they did not even realize.

102 THINGS GET CUT; IT HAPPENS A LOT

There are many reasons that It happens. Ensure you or the staff that did the work understand why it got cut. Often, it has little to do with the quality of the item and more to do with it no longer being helpful to the storytelling that is occurring. The item can still be put in stock, used for future shows, and included in your portfolio of work. I had a bench I built early in my career for a devised piece that was complicated and hard to make; I thought it was beautiful by the time I finished it and sent it to rehearsal. The next day, it was back in the shop, and when I asked the prop supervisor why it was there, he told me it had been cut from the show. I was devastated. He talked to me about it and explained that they had changed the scene and the bench wasn't needed anymore. It took me a long while to get over it. When I finally did, I realized it wasn't about the quality of the bench but about how it was used in the piece that really mattered in the long run. That bench is still in my portfolio.

103 KISS – KEEP IT SIMPLE STUPID

We have lots of new-fangled technology at our disposal, and there are times when the 3D printer is the answer, or adding a motor and an Arduino control unit makes the prop effect work amazingly well, but more often than not, a more straightforward solution is probably just as, if not more, effective. Shows sometimes run for a long time, and the props need to be low maintenance and hold up to the abuse of the production. Keep it simple; find the simplest and most effective way of doing something; it will almost always save you time and headaches. Do effects with the least number of moving parts and the fewest electronic components, and ensure the components you use are easy to get to and easily replaceable.

In a production of *Coconuts*, they wanted a cash register where the drawer would open when a button was pushed, and a bell would ring. Due to size limitations and period appropriateness, we determined we had to build this prop. We created a realistic-looking cash register on a smaller scale than a real one due to the size of the counter it had to sit on. We used keys off an old typewriter as our buttons. Rubber bands and a simple spring latch provided the resistance to hold the drawer closed, and we used simple springs to pop it open. The drawer itself served a mechanical function; as it slid out, we had a small metal extension piece that hit and rang the bell. We made the back of the cash register removable using easy-to-remove and replace pins. This made opening the cash register easy and accessing the moving parts and mechanisms inside. This made it quick and straightforward to replace a rubber band if it ever snapped (it only happened once in our 40+ performance run).

In a more recent production of *The Play That Goes Wrong*, we knew we had to keep the tricks simple and repeatable for our 60+ performance run. After much research and a great deal of discussion, we decided not to use a single motor, solenoid, or pneumatic ram for any of the effects. The crew manually controlled everything. We used high-strength industrial magnets that would work through our ¼" wood flat-facing material to hold items to the walls; when they needed to fall, the crew removed the magnets, and the objects fell to the floor. With a nearly invisible spike onstage for the actors and a pronounced spike on the back for the crew, the actors could hold the items on the walls, and the crew could reset the magnets from the back to allow the items to stay on the walls again magically. Another great thing about this option is that it allowed us to move objects around during tech as we worked the bits to ensure the actors could reach everything and stay safe. It didn't require running new electrical or airlines or drilling multiple holes in the set. The safety, repeatability, and ease of use of the effect have to be taken into consideration early in the process and must be refined and developed in association with the process of getting the play on its feet, but if there is clear communication of expectations and desired outcomes from the get-go then keeping the effects simple will often prove the most effective method.

104 DON'T GET BOGGED DOWN IN MINUTIA

There are so many details in every production that if you start down the rabbit hole of making everything perfect, real, and authentic, you will end up spiraling out of control and very likely won't have all the props and dressing for the show ready on time. Talk to the director and the designer(s) early in the process so you understand the focus of the production and the essential aspects of it. Work to make those items and moments really shine and sparkle. Again, think about the storytelling aspect of our craft and work within that. The information from the director is to make sure the emphasis and detail are in the props that propel that storytelling forward. This will also benefit the audience. If everything is detailed to the Nth degree, then it can also be hard for them to know where to focus. This is also true regarding the physical work of creating the props themselves. I am a big proponent of texture and details on objects, and once you have put the time and energy into adding that level of finish, you want to make sure it reads so it can be appreciated. To help that texture pop (read), you often add some highlight and shadow to the objects. However, if you detail every item on stage to the same level and then highlight and shadow all of that texture on every item on stage, the audience will get exhausted just looking at the props because there will be so much detail everywhere they won't know what is important or where to look/focus. Pick your details wisely to assist in storytelling, and work hard to turn those critical storytelling props into hero props (even if they don't get a zoomed close-up).

105 DETAILS ARE IMPORTANT

That being said, specific details can be crucial to a production, and you want to make sure those are right. This is particularly true in smaller venues where the audience is close to the action or, in some cases, even walking across the set to get to their seats. Years ago, I did a production of Nixon's Nixon, a play about the final few days of Nixon's presidency. It was in an intimate theater in the round. We had a presidential desk, and on it was a perpetual calendar. I set the calendar to the day the events in the play took place; since this play is based on historical events, the exact date(s) are known. When I arrived for the first day of tech, I noticed the date had been changed. I reset it to the appropriate date. After the dinner break, I again saw the date had been changed. I noted the date it was set on and again returned it to the correct date for the production. It was again different the next day, but I saw it was the exact date it had been the day before. On a break, I approached the actor playing Nixon and asked him if he had changed the calendar; he said he had, and the date showing was his wife's birthday. I told him I appreciated the sentiment, but that as we were in such close proximity to the audience, maybe we should set it to the date that the play took place, and feeling a bit chagrined, he admitted that might be a good idea, I reset it, and he left the calendar alone for the run of the show.

106 AESTHETIC DESIRE/VISION VS. PHYSICAL REALITY/LIMITATIONS

The battle between the aesthetic desire of the director and designer versus the physical reality and limitations of production is constant and one that we can't always win. The director or designer has an idea of exactly how they want the prop, set piece, or costume to work in the moment to create the storytelling they are after, but often, physics or physical limitations don't allow for that to occur in precisely the way the director or designer envisioned. We need to understand the desire and reasoning behind the vision for the moment and then work to offer the best possible option(s) within the physical world's limits to make the moment happen. We often try to get to that director or designer's vision by asking them to describe the movie in their head and how they see the moment/scene playing out. Once we begin creating that vision, or the compromise vision that we all have worked out based on the spatial, financial, and labor resources available, we are on the right track. If, as that process begins, we realize there are issues with creating the whole vision, we immediately communicate to those higher up in the production that we are running into some issues and working on solutions. We can't be silent and hope they cut the bit. We ask questions, explain what we are doing to solve the problem, explain the limitations, and work together to find an agreeable solution that maintains as much of the vision as possible within the limitations. Early communication is always good to help alleviate some of these issues and concerns.

Working on a recent production of *Romeo and Juliet*, the designer sent in a drawing of the bed for Juliet and a unit for Friar Lawrence's cell. We have been working in that theater for several years, and looking at both units, I realized the dimensions would be a problem. While both units would fit onstage, there was no good path to get them there. They wouldn't fit through the backstage doorways to get to the stage. We were repping this show with *A Midsummer Night's Dream*, so at least one, if not both, would need to move into storage every couple of days to allow for the other production. We remeasured all our doorway openings and sent that information to the designer. We worked with her to adjust the size of both units to allow for clearance of the units through our backstage spaces. While adjusting the bed's height, width, and length from the initial design, it still felt large and imposing (as intended) when onstage. We made it useable rather than leaving it on the loading dock outside the theater, never being able to get onstage, or having to do a major rebuild at tech when we got to the theater and learned the bed wouldn't fit through the doorways.

The dollar bill – not a tip or trick, just an insight

When I was a freshman in college many years ago, I was required to take a class titled Artist in Society taught by one of the acting/directing faculty members named Michael Burnham. The purpose of the class, as explained on the first day, was to give us topics of conversation when we were in public that did not all revolve around theater. My take on the class was that it showed us there was more to life than theater and our jobs, but that is a philosophical discussion for another time. On the first day of class, Professor Burnham asked if anyone had a dollar bill and if he could borrow it. Some first-year student offered up a dollar, and Michael took it from them. He then quickly counted the number of people in the room and began to rip the dollar bill into pieces, the exact number of pieces that represented everyone in the room. As he did this, he explained that each of us had come to school to learn a specific craft or skill, be it scenic design, acting, props, lighting, etc., but those skills by themselves were not enough. Theater is a collaborative art. If each of us worked our craft by ourselves without interaction or collaboration, what we would have would have little to no value, much like the piece of the dollar bill that he handed each of us during the class. But if we each took our craft and worked with, collaborated with, the others in the room, then what we created would have value, much like if we each took our piece of the dollar bill and combined it with all the other parts, then we would have something of value, $1. Just as if we all worked together, we would have a theatrical event, a play, an opera, or the like that would provide our audiences with a moment in time that changed them in a perceived or non-perceived way. I have never forgotten that sentiment, and I still have that piece of the dollar bill in my little box of knick-knacks. I share this idea with my staff each year (not always destroying US currency), but on occasion, I create that visual representation of the part that each of us plays in creating live entertainment (Image 10.1).

Image 10.1 A photo of my chunk of the dollar bill from my artist in society class.

Source: Photo by the author.

Tips from the wider world of props

Eleven

As I said in the introduction, I only know some things about props. I learn new things daily and hope my career continues to give me opportunities to explore and add to my knowledge. One of the best ways I have found to continue the learning process is to watch others in the same field and see how they deal with situations and opportunities. I have met many exceptional individuals over the years. I picked a handful that I have known for a long time and that work in different aspects of the entertainment business, and I asked each of them to fill out a four-question survey. I am including their responses in their entirety here so that you can gain some of the same wisdom that I have from them.

They answered these four questions:

1. Give me a brief bio of yourself.
2. What is one physical tip or trick that has helped you in your career?
3. What is one piece of advice you would give to someone in this career field?
4. Is there anything else you would like to share?

107 ASHLEY FLOWERS

Bio: I (she/her) am an actor, producer, content creator, and prop artisan/master living in Chicago, IL, with my wife. I have worked for Netflix and NBC. I have also produced two shorts in Los Angeles and am currently working on my third. I studied props at Yale University and made my transition from theater to film when I moved to California. I studied acting at Steppenwolf West and The Groundlings. I have enjoyed my career going back and forth, from behind the camera to in front of it. I have a passion for creating films, and my goal is to create more queer films that are appropriately represented on and off-screen. As an actor, I love playing roles of characters who are typically misunderstood by society, have been struggling mentally, or maybe just don't fit into society's norms. I love to understand humans and their backgrounds. I am also a proud member of SAG and IATSE.

Physical Tip: My side pack (an oversized fanny pack) has been very helpful in having all my tools near me, especially when I am running around set.

Piece of advice: Always be willing to learn, and remember there are no right answers. Every problem has multiple solutions. Be kind to everyone.

Anything Else: Props help bring the story to life not only for the audience but also for the actor. It's important that they are as realistic as possible to help the actor stay in the world. A good prop blends into the world and makes sense.

108 KATIE BLACKBURN

Bio: After graduating from the University of Louisville with a BFA, I worked in the theater community for five more years. I was a Set Carpenter, Props Artisan, and Prop Master. I eventually transitioned into film, where I've worked in Construction as a Grip, Stylist, Prop Master, Art Director, and Production Designer. My time in theater prepared me with a myriad of skills that have made me a competitive hire and creative problem solver. If you have a wild idea, I can probably figure out how to make it happen. Please don't ask me to describe what I do for a living, you wouldn't believe it. A lot of my time these days is spent handing props to people called "celebrities."

Physical Tip: Label everything with paper tape and a Sharpie. There are a lot of props and prop-building materials that look like trash. I've watched Grips nearly eat prop food onset and Production Assistants nearly throw away prop trash.

Piece of advice: Ask people how they make a thing. Electricians, Cooks, Blacksmiths, Rocket Scientists. There's something to learn from most processes. Be curious, and think critically.

Other wisdom: Keep everything in perspective. How important is the thing you're consumed by? If you can't pass your own standards, recognize that. Sometimes, done is better than good; you probably did an amazing job anyway. Don't be lazy; learn everything, but also balance.

109 LORI HARRISON

Bio: Head of the Properties Department at San Francisco Opera since 1999; other assorted jobs before that at Greater Miami Opera, Santa Fe Opera, and Chautauqua Opera. Film, commercial, and modelmaking work on a few features, TV series, and at Industrial Light and Magic. Member of IATSE Local 16. Educated (a million years ago) at Penn State University and the University of Pennsylvania

Physical Tip: When presenting to a director and/or designer, try to have more than one idea or "how-to" to present. That allows you to if YOU have a preference, make it a little more finished or somehow emphasized while allowing THEM to be the ones making the choice. Be prepared for them not to pick your favorite, though: it is a collaborative process!

Piece of advice: OPEN eyes, OPEN ears, OPEN mind: there is ALWAYS ALWAYS more to learn: keep observing, learning, taking in. You will have so much more to give out in the way of ideas, quality of product, and community in which you are working! If you are in school, take advantage of opportunities to learn things that you think will be useful. You will use it all: languages, history, art, math, science, properties of materials, literature, and music. It will all be a part of your career.

Anything Else: Two things I would like to share: (1) A theory about the difference between propping/set dressing for film and for stage: Stage is a little more "Outside-In": the picture is created by a designer, and the look is from the outside: palette, period, concept, etc.... For film, propping is a little more "Inside-Out" or character-driven. One doesn't know where the camera might end up, and you – as the set dresser – are choosing details that come from the characters in that space (books they are reading? choices in neatness? furniture choices, or objects in the space?) You are creating the space that is lived in. (2) Props involves EVERYBODY, more so than any other discipline in theater: we deal with performers, other technicians, producers, managers, wardrobe and costumes, lighting and sound, and even the audience community. That's what makes it the most fun part of theater.

110 KELLY KREUTSBERG

Bio: Props Director at Milwaukee Rep. Former Props Manager of Repertory Theatre of St Louis and Adjunct Faculty of Webster University. She spent many summers with Ben and Marielle in Cedar City, learning all their tips and tricks.

Physical Tip: Picking machine for foliage How to use math to find the size of things in photos How to twist the fabric with the pliers to pull staples out of upholstery. I can write a bible on how not to build a chicken.

Piece of advice: Be bold and ask questions of everyone you meet. Make the call to the specialist. It might make their day to teach you about their specialty, whether it is African Tribal Weaponry or taxidermy. This also goes for asking other departments. You might not know that the draper has a collection of antique dolls or that the board op has his own CNC machine.

Anything Else: Props is all about solving problems and continual learning. As long as you have a desire to learn, you can be a props person.

111 NATHAN MICHAEL

Bio: is a former properties professional, having most recently spent over ten years in Las Vegas working for Cirque du Soleil in various roles, including Head of the Properties Department for *Viva Elvis* and *Zarkana* at Aria Resort and Casino, as well as Head of Carpentry and Props for *Zumanity* at New York, New York Hotel and Casino. Prior to his stint in Las Vegas, Nathan worked in various regional theater prop departments. He taught courses at the University of Missouri, Kansas City, and the University of Illinois at Urbana-Champaign.

Physical Tip: Something that has helped me is when I had downtime to take broken objects apart. Learning how objects worked or failed has helped when designing new props.

Piece of advice: Accept the fact that you are never going to have enough time to do everything that you want. Remember, stuff is cheaper than people, so always buy what you can. When building a prop, realize that someone somewhere builds and sells the same thing. Consider buying it from them. Directors and designers don't care about your staff. Don't be like directors or designers. Remember, it's just a show. You are not curing cancer.

112 EIMER MURPHY

Bio: A stage manager who was handy with props gradually turned prop maker and now Prop Master of The Abbey Theatre.

Physical Tip: Latex and Muslin scrim over carved upholstery foam. You can make nearly anything out of this combo, and it's practically indestructible.

Piece of advice: Talk to actors all the way through the process. Let them handle the thing, test it out, and take their notes.

Anything Else: Good props can really support performance. Be proud of your contribution.

113   ADRIANE "BINKY" DONLEY

Bio: is the Properties Director at Krannert Center for the Performing Arts and the Chair of the Properties Design and Management MFA program at the University of Illinois Urbana Champaign. Previously, she was an Assistant Professor of Props and Scenic Arts at Ithaca College. Her time as an artisan was spent at the Heritage Repertory Theatre, Seaside Musical Theatre, Virginia Shakespeare Festival, the Alley Theater, and the Actors Theater of Louisville.

Physical Tip: I always use a 1/2" seam allowance on all of my upholstery projects, such as draperies, pillows, and seat cushions. It just makes the math easier. Upholstery fabric is often expensive and can be intimidating for people just starting out. So, I figured by making the math easier, you're less likely to make an error when either figuring out how much fabric you need or where to cut each piece. The other reason is that if you use 1/2" as your seam allowance and you're adding piping to a pillow and such, the measurement from the stitch line of the piping to the unfinished edge of the piping is about 1/2". Therefore, when you pin your piping to the fabric, you're just lining up the edges and not trying to insert it to a different measurement. It makes your life so much easier, and the project finishes faster. Another tip that is more common sense than a tip is to do a sample for whatever project you're doing. Young artists don't realize that this is part of the process and not a thing you have to do because you don't know. The old-timers are still learning, too, and yes, we know more. But we still do a sample.

Piece of advice: Everyone's path is different and don't compare what you're doing to others; instead, take it as a learning opportunity. I've learned so much by watching others work, asking them questions, and then asking for their critique on my projects. It's not a competition; no one is keeping score, and ego has no place in a prop shop.

Anything Else: One of the two biggest lessons I've learned in this industry is that a little kindness goes a long way, and if you want something, ask. Don't be intimidated. Also, ask more than one person (in case you get pushback by the first person you ask.) Over the years, colleagues have said to me several times, "How did you get that? How do you know about that?" I was nice, persistent, and I asked.

114   PATRICK DRONE

Bio: I originally went to college to study industrial education. That's correct. My goal in life was to be a high school shop teacher. I started doing theater and became hooked. It had all the challenges I was looking for. Since leaving school, I have worked in theater from coast to coast. Two of the strangest non theater jobs I have had were as a Shipfitter on nuclear reactors for submarines at Newport News Shipbuilding and as an Antique Vehicle Specialist for the Henry Ford Museum/ Greenfield Village. There are more similarities between the Ford Model T and a submarine than you would think. I have always enjoyed teaching and building props because it blurs the line between art and engineering.

Physical Tip: (1). Get information (prop lists, renderings, research) as early as you can. This will help in seeing what items can and cannot change during the rehearsal process. (2) When giving designers or directors options, always give three: one that you think is the best, one that will do and one that is an easy reject. Their reactions to these three choices will help establish your communication styles together. (3) Remember that it's their vision of the show you're helping to produce, not your own. (4) A bad prop on a great set will stick out just as much as a great prop on a bad set.

Piece of advice: (1). Always build for your closest audience. Props can then be used in any space. (2) Don't let perfection stand in the way of done.

Anything Else: Learn, Learn, Learn. The more you know and the more you grow, the happier you will be.

115   JIM GUY

Bio: I've been a Props Director, Props Designer, and Props Educator for 43 years. I have freelanced and done theater, opera, TV, a little film, commercial and print work. I directed the MFA program in

Theatrical Properties Management and Design at the University of IL at Urbana-Champaign, served as President of the Society of Props Managers (S*P*M) for 16 years and as Properties Director at Milwaukee Repertory Theater for 24 seasons. I recently retired from the Rep to resume freelance Prop Design, teaching, and writing. I was born in a log cabin. I never tell a lie.

Physical Tip: Frequent and direct communication is the key to a smooth and efficient process. One email often does nothing more than make three more emails necessary. I make a point of speaking with Stage Management daily before rehearsal to address notes and pose questions. I make an effort to establish a dialog with all actors regarding their props and business, familiarizing myself with their process and keeping Stage Management informed regarding the content of those conversations.

Piece of advice: Never approach a problem with only one solution in mind. You should always have a Plan B ready to put into action.

Anything Else: Magnets are usually the answer.

116 KEVIN WILLIAMS

Bio: a recovering actor and L.A. native has spent over two decades as a designer, fabricator, and consultant for clients such as Walt Disney Imagineering, ABC, Buena Vista Pictures, HUB Network, Red 5 Studios, and Twentieth Century Fox, among others. Notably, he was the resident Production Designer for the interactive theater company Delusion for over seven years. Immersive credits include Lies Within (2014), His Crimson Queen (2016), Horror Rewind (2017), Lies Within VR (2017), The Blue Blade (2018), and Reaper's Remorse (2021.) Kevin is the Prop Department Supervisor for UCLA's School of Theater, Film & Television and lives in Orange County with his incredible family.

Physical Tip: Regardless of the project's scale, don't skimp on the finer details. It's when you least expect it that they will matter most. It's even more important in immersive/experiential events when your audience is up close and personal with 95% of your work. Some of my favorite work was designing and building all of the hero props that traveled with the audience through an immersive event. Creating something so detailed that they get to handle it so intimately gives them a depth of realism and a sense of agency on an otherwise linear path. It's very satisfying to know that such a small element can play such a big role in how little or how much an audience member enjoys an experience.

Piece of advice: Remain open in the times when you are faced with your most difficult and seemingly insurmountable tasks. Don't be afraid to take a break to clear your head and refocus your energies to find the elusive solution. Look for small victories to keep you going, and always trust the process.

Anything Else: The scope of work and expectations of props for a modern audience and team of creatives has grown exponentially over the last few decades. I've learned to not be afraid to offer up ideas and advocate for yourself and your team by being a constant voice at the table. Props is a unique and highly challenging career path, but so, so rewarding for the right individuals who are up to the challenge. Another thing I've come to discover, after more than 20 years, is that it's not about the hard skills in a shop that make a person successful in Props. It's about the soft skills like problem-solving and relationship-building. Master those, and everything else falls into place.

117 CRAIG GRIGG

Bio: I've worked as a Specialty Propmaker in New York City for over 20 years, designing and/or fabricating specialty mechanical and electrical items, as well as trick and illusion props, puppets, and practical effects. I've built sofas that eject vomit, sofas that shoot blood, and sofas that levitate and catapult their own cushions. I've built brassieres that squirt water, body parts that squirt urine, and a chorus line of dancing animatronic priapic appendages. I've built a well-known talking gingerbread cookie puppet and breakaway props for a well-known puppet who talks about cookies. And in addition to these notable projects, a mountain of boring stuff that no one will ever remember but was apparently worth losing sleep over at the time. As a Freelance Individual or with various companies, I have contributed work to over 75 Broadway shows, as well as Off-Broadway, Television, Film, Dance, Opera, Visual Art, and Magic. Before moving to New York, I worked and honed my craft in Regional Theater, Summer Stock Theater, Community Theater, and, most importantly, Small Town Beauty Pageants. I graduated High School from the North Carolina School of Science and Mathematics and received a BA in Theater from the intimate and excellent Catawba College.

Physical Tip: As prop makers, we are often asked to build something seemingly impossible, or more often, something positively ridiculous, usually by tomorrow, and always with little to no money. These challenges often seem so difficult that we immediately assume the solution must be difficult as well. I have found that it's important, when attempting to meet such challenges with creative solutions, to remember that being creative does not mean creating everything from scratch. Creativity is resourcefulness, and knowing what resources are available is key. You do not need to reinvent the wheel with every project. Often, pieces of the solution already exist, and in many cases, you will find that you've solved very similar problems before. The key is to know what you've done before that worked and what parts of that solution are readily available. To this end, I have two tips. First, being the analog person that I am, I always keep a notebook with me when working – an actual paper notebook – single subject, sewn binding – the black and white speckled composition variety. I use it as a daily diary and keep notes, sketches, dimensions, weights, and material or hardware part numbers written down. I keep quick notes of progress and build information such as cut lists and order-of-operation, which can come in very handy when a prop is inevitably destroyed onstage or when a show implausibly goes well, and multiple productions are built to tour. Since the pages are not meant to be removed, everything stays in chronological order – a little time capsule of production mayhem that you can return to when you need that special spring-loaded whatever again. Second, become familiar with the McMaster-Carr supply company's online catalog. Local hardware stores and home centers are great, but they only stock what people generally need and buy – not specialty hardware. The McMaster catalog is a virtual encyclopedia of what hardware and materials – from the mundane to the medical – exist and are ready to ship. Everything is specified by its physical properties rather than brand name or price, so you can search "quick release pin" or "food grade grease" without knowing the trade name for any of it. It is an education in pipe size, screw pitches, and adhesive properties. Small quantities and sizes of most products are available for experimentation, so you don't have to buy a truckload of something just to find out it's not what you need. As a caveat – it is not inexpensive, but the products are all high quality, and their return policies are very fair.

Knowing what specialty hinge or space-age epoxy can be incorporated into your project is great, and knowing that it will arrive on schedule is a lifesaver.

Piece of advice: Props are often the last piece of the show puzzle, shaped and determined by every other part of the production, so it's important to know as much about all the other disciplines as possible. Learning as much as you can about how the other Design departments work, as well as understanding the needs of Stage Managers, Directors, and, of course, Actors, will help inform the way props are built, used, and ultimately, destroyed. Learn about things outside of the theater. Plays are generally (and fortunately) not about theater technicians, so a broad understanding of the world at large is necessary to be part of good storytelling. Be kind to people and keep a healthy perspective on your work. The Performing Arts is a collaborative field, full of passion and creativity, but generally devoid of extra time and money. Things can become stressful, but never forget to be kind and never forget that it's just a show.

Words of the trade (Glossary)

Twelve

These words (while not a definitive list) are words that we tend to use often in props. Many are not specific to props but also are not in everyday use in the world at large. Knowing them can help you navigate the world of prop building. There are words that prop people use regularly that are not in everyday use but are essential to know. The glossary will provide these words, definitions, and some historical context or other tidbit to allow the reader to better understand them and their use in theatrical prop work. All basic definitions are taken from the Merriam-Webster online dictionary, additional definition work, or historical data (in italics) provided by me.

1. Andirons (noun) – a pair of metal supports for firewood used on a hearth and made of a horizontal bar mounted on short legs with usually a vertical shaft surmounting the front end.
2. Antimacassar (noun) – a cover to protect the back or arms of furniture; *A small cloth, often of lace or tatting (a doily) placed over the backs or arms of chairs to prevent soiling of the permanent fabric. This comes from a men's hair oil brand popular in the 1800's, Macassar oil. This oil stained the fabric of the furniture, so doilies were placed on the furniture to soak up the oil as they could be removed and laundered.*
3. Baton (noun) – a staff borne as a symbol of office.
4. Bergere (noun) – an upholstered armchair of an 18th-century style having an exposed wood frame.
5. Bier (noun) – a stand on which a corpse or coffin is placed often for transporting it to the grave.
6. Billy club (noun) – a heavy, usually wooden club, specifically a police officer's club.
7. Bobeche (noun) – a usually glass collar on a candle socket to catch drippings or on a candlestick or chandelier to hold suspended glass prisms; *originally, all bobeches were used to catch wax so it would not*

drop from a chandelier, sconce, or candlestick, as the world transitioned first to oil and gas and then to electric lighting the bobeche became more of a decorative item.

8. Bolster (noun) – a long, narrow pillow or cushion, often cylindrical in shape.
9. Bookplate (noun) – a book owner's identification label that is usually pasted to the inside front cover of a book.
10. Bota bag – *a bag made of leather used to carry wine or other liquids; also, a wineskin.*
11. Broadside (noun) – a sizable sheet of paper printed on one side; *a precursor to the modern newspaper.*
12. Buckler (noun) – a small round shield held by a handle at arm's length; *this type of shield is gripped in the fist, appropriate for hand-to-hand combat.*
13. Cambric (noun) – a fine, thin white linen fabric; *in modern use, a synthetic material also referred to as dust cover used to cover the underside of furniture to keep dust and debris out and to cover the springs, webbing, and other parts of the upholstered furniture.*
14. Candelabra (noun) – a branched candlestick or lamp with several lights.
15. Carafe (noun) – a bottle with a flaring lip used to hold beverages, especially wine.
16. Cartouche (noun) – an ornate or ornamental frame; an oval or oblong figure (as on ancient Egyptian monuments) enclosing a sovereign's name.
17. Chaise/Chaise Longue (noun) – a long reclining chair; *an upholstered sofa in the shape of a chair that is long enough to support the legs.*
18. Chamber pot (noun) – a bedroom vessel for urination and defecation.
19. Charger (noun) – a large flat dish or platter; *a decorative plate used to dress up dinner tables for special events. The charger is placed on the table as part of the pre-dinner set-up and is often left for the entire meal. As the courses are served the individual plates, bowls, and the like are placed on the charger at each place setting.*
20. Chesterfield (noun) – a Davenport, usually with upright armrests.
21. Chifforobe (noun) – a combination of wardrobe and chest of drawers.
22. Chuppah (noun) – a canopy under which the bride and groom stand during a Jewish wedding ceremony.
23. Clerestory (noun) – an outside wall of a room or building that rises above an adjoining roof and contains widows.

24. Coal Scuttle (noun) – a metal pail for holding and carrying coal, typically having a bail and a sloping lip for ease in pouring.
25. Corbel (noun) – an architectural member that projects from within a wall and supports a weight, particularly one that is stepped upward and outward from a vertical surface.
26. Couch (noun) – an article of furniture for sitting or reclining.
27. Counterpane (noun) – a usually ornamental cloth cover for a bed; *a bedspread.*
28. Crozier (noun) – a staff resembling a shepherd's crook carried by bishops and abbots as a symbol of office.
29. Cudgel (noun) – a short heavy club.
30. Cuspidor (noun) – a place for spitting (see Spittoon) *from the Portuguese language.*
31. Davenport (noun) – a small compact writing desk; a large upholstered sofa often convertible into a bed.
32. Distress (verb) – to mar (something, such as clothing or wood) deliberately to give an effect of age.
33. Divan (noun) – a large couch, usually without a back or arms, often designed for use as a bed.
34. Dustcover (noun) – a cover (as of cloth or plastic) used to protect furniture or equipment from dust (see Cambric).
35. Dustjacket (noun) – a paper cover for a book.
36. Ear trumpet (noun) – a trumpet-shaped instrument used for collecting and intensifying sounds to aid a person with defective hearing.
37. Ephemera (noun) – paper items (such as posters, broadsides, and tickets) that were originally meant to be discarded after use but have since become collectible; something of no lasting significance; *transitory written or printed matter not intended to be retained or preserved.*
38. Escutcheon (noun) – a protective or ornamental plate or flange (as around a keyhole).
39. Ewer (noun) – a vase-shaped pitcher or jug.
40. Finial (noun) – a usually foliated ornament forming an upper extremity, especially in Gothic architecture; a crowning ornament or detail (such as a decorative knob); *a decorative element used on the ends of flagpoles, curtain rods, and the like.*
41. Frog (noun) – a leather or fabric loop attached to a belt to hold a weapon or tool.

42. Gimp (noun) – an ornamental flat braid or round cord used as a trimming.
43. Gonfalon (noun) – a flag that hangs from a crosspiece or frame.
44. Halberd (noun) – a weapon especially of the 15th and 16th centuries consisting typically of a battle-ax and pike mounted on a handle about six feet long.
45. Hassock (noun) – a cushion for kneeling; a padded cushion or low stool that serves as a seat or leg rest.
46. Highboy (noun) – a tall chest of drawers with a legged base.
47. Inglenook (noun) – a nook by a large open fireplace; a bench or settle occupying this nook.
48. Jabot (noun) – a decorative window treatment that drapes vertically from the sides of the window, usually as pleats or gathers.
49. Jardinière (noun) – an ornamental stand for plants or flowers; a large usually ceramic flowerpot holder.
50. Lectern (noun) – a stand used to support a book or script in a convenient position for a standing reader or speaker.
51. Life preserver (noun) – a hand weapon typically consisting of a piece of leather0enclosed metal with a strap or springy shaft for a handle.
52. Litter (noun) – a covered and curtained couch provided with shafts and used for carrying a single passenger; a device (such as a stretcher) for carrying a sick or injured person; *a human-powered transport usually with poles for lifting and carrying a single passenger.*
53. Lounge (noun) – a long couch.
54. Lowboy (noun) – a chest or side table about three feet (one meter) high with drawers and usually with cabriole legs.
55. LP record (noun) – an analog sound storage medium, a record format characterized by a speed of 33+1/3 rpm; a 12- or 10-inch diameter; and a vinyl composition disk.
56. Mullion (noun) – a slender vertical member that forms a division between units of a window, door, or screen or is used decoratively.
57. Nap (noun) – a hairy, fuzzy, or downy surface (as on a fabric).
58. Nib (noun) – the sharpened point of a quill pen; each of the two divisions of a pen point.
59. Oculus (noun) – a circular or oval window; a circular opening at the top of a dome.

60. Oeil-de-boeuf (noun) – a French phrase for oculus – directly translates to "ox's eye".
61. Ottoman (noun) – an upholstered, often overstuffed seat or couch, usually without a back; an overstuffed footstool.
62. Partner's Desk (noun) – a large desk with an open kneehole which allows use of the desk by two people seated opposite each other.
63. Pen point (noun) – a small thin, convex metal device that tapers to a split point, fits into a holder, and is used for writing and drawing.
64. Pianoforte (noun) – an early form of the piano originating in the 18th or early 19th centuries and having a smaller range and softer timbre than a modern piano.
65. Plinth (noun) – the lowest member of a base; a block upon which the moldings of an architrave or trim are stopped at the bottom; a usually square block serving as a base.
66. Plumb Line (noun) – a line (as of cord) that has at one end a weight (such as a plumb bob) and is used especially to determine verticality.
67. Podium (noun) – a dais especially for an orchestral conductor (see also Lectern).
68. Polaroid (noun) – trademark; a light polarizing material; a camera that produces developed pictures.
69. Pouffe (noun) – (see Ottoman); *a piece of furniture used as a footstool or low seat; completely covered in fabric with no visible legs.*
70. Pram (noun) – a small four-wheeled carriage, often with a folding top for pushing a baby around in; also called a baby buggy; popular during the Victorian era.
71. Prie-Dieu (noun) – a kneeling bench designed for use by a person at prayer and fitted with a raised shelf on which the elbows or a book may be rested; *in their early use they were created for well-to-do individuals for use in their private chapels, within their homes or on their estate.*
72. Putto (singular) Putti (plural) (noun) – a figure of an infant boy, especially in European art of the Renaissance.
73. Quill (noun) – the hollow horny shaft of a feather, *particularly one of the large stiff feathers of the wing or tail or portion thereof used for writing or drawing with ink or a similar fluid.*
74. Salt Cellar (noun) – a dish or container for storing salt unlike a salt shaker, a cellar allows you to pinch a collection of salt grains

in your fingers for food seasoning; *also, sometimes referred to as a salt dish, master salt, open salt, salt dip, standing salt, or salt pig.*

75. Salver (noun) – a small tray-like object without handles and smaller than a standard tray, used in formal circumstances; *calling cards were often presented on salvers.*

76. Samovar (noun) – an urn with a spigot at its base, used especially in Russia, to boil water for tea; an urn similar to a Russian Samovar with a device for heating the contents.

77. Savonarola chair (noun) – a folding X-shaped chair of Italian Renaissance style that has interlaced curved slats pivoted at their intersections; often *referred to as an X chair; the earliest versions folded up to make them easier to transport.*

78. Schmatta (noun) – Yiddish for rag.

79. Sconce (noun) – a bracket candlestick or group of candlesticks; an electric light fixture patterned on a candle sconce.

80. Scuttle (noun) – a shallow open basket for carrying something (such as grain or garden produce).

81. Settee (noun) – a long seat with a back; a medium sized sofa with arms and a back.

82. Settle (noun) – a wooden bench with arms, a high solid back, and an enclosed foundation which can be used as a chest.

83. Sofa (noun) – a long upholstered seat usually with arms and a back and often convertible into a bed.

84. Spittoon (noun) – a receptacle for spit (see Cuspidor); *especially by users of tobacco.*

85. Splat (noun) – a single flat thin often ornamental member of a back of a chair.

86. Spurtle (noun) – a wooden stick for stirring porridge.

87. Stylus (noun) – an instrument for writing, marking, or incising: such as an instrument used by the ancients in writing on clay or waxed tablets; a hard-pointed pen-shaped instrument for marking on stencils used in a reproducing machine; a pen-shaped pointing device used for entering data (such as positional information from a graphics tablet) into a computer.

88. Tallboy (noun) – a double chest of drawers usually with the upper section slightly smaller than the lower (also called a Highboy).

89. Tchotchke (noun) – a small trivial article usually intended for ornament (see Trinket); *a decorative item or souvenir, usually of no particular value, this is a Yiddish word.*
90. Terrarium (noun) – a usually transparent enclosure for keeping or raising plants or small animals (such as turtles) indoors.
91. Tete-a-Tete (noun) – a short piece of furniture (such as a sofa) intended to seat two persons especially facing each other; *a bench or sofa that allows two people to talk face to face.*
92. Thunder stick (noun) – a slat of wood tied to the end of a thong and making an intermittent roaring sound when whirled that is used especially by Australian aborigines in religious rites or among western peoples as a children's toy.
93. Tie-back (noun) – a decorative strip of fabric or cord, typically used for holding an open curtain off to the side of the window.
94. Trinket (noun) – a small ornament (such as a jewel or ring); a small article of equipment; a thing of little value (see Tchotchke).
95. Trivet (noun) – a usually metal or wooden stand often with short feet for use under a hot dish.
96. Trompe l'oeil (noun) – a style of painting in which objects are depicted with photographically realistic detail; something that misleads or deceives the senses; French origin – translates to: deceives the eye; *a paint treatment that provides highlight and shadow and creates the feeling of a 3-D object all on a 2-D plane.*
97. Trug (noun) – a shallow rectangular gardening basket.
98. Truncheon (noun) – a police officer's billy club (see Baton).
99. Tuffet (noun) – a low seat.
100. Valance (noun) – a drapery hung along the edge of a bed, table, altar, canopy, or shelf; a short drapery or wood or metal frame used a decorative heading to conceal the top of curtains and fixtures.
101. Vivarium (noun) – a terrarium used especially for small animals.
102. Welt (or Welting) (noun) – a doubled edge, strip, insert, or seam (as on a garment) for ornament or reinforcement.
103. Zany (noun) – a subordinate clown or acrobat in old comedies who mimics ludicrously the tricks of the principal; a servile follower; one who acts the buffoon to amuse others; *the bauble (often in the shape of a jester) that this type of person carries when they perform.*

Index

3D printer 99, 101, 103, 146, 150
5-in-1 tool 50–51

Alsace/Rhone bottle 114
angles 22–23

ball chain, using it to wire light fixtures 67–68
barrel 107–108
beer mug 109, 113
bias tape 34–38
blind stitch 24
bolt threads, cleaning up 7
Bordeaux bottle 114
bowline 134–136
box pleats 40–42
breakaway(s) 72, 102, 145, 162
Burgundy bottle 114
button(s), fabric covered 44–46
button maker 90
button making 44
button tufted 44, 48, 92

cask 107–108
center-finding jig 1–2
centimeters, conversion to 11, 20–21, 35
chain busting pliers 85–86
charger 117–119
cling wrap *see* stretch wrap
clove hitch 132–134
CNC router 104–106
Collins glass 109–110

colored hot glue for sealing wax 63–65
cordial glass 109–110
cosplay foam *see* EVA foam
coupe (glass) 109, 111
crackle finish/crackle glaze 55–56
currency, printing faux 72

date things 138, 140
deckling 69
dessert wine glass 109, 112
die-cutting machine 88–91
distressing furniture 57–62
distressing paper 69
double old fashioned (glass) 109
drapes and curtains: determining fullness 38–39; pleating styles 39–40; quick fullness 42–44
Dremel (quick release) 84–85
drink glasses 108–113

e-cigarette(s) 81
enlarging, finding percentages 15–18
envelope sizes, international 121–122
envelope sizes, North America 120–122
EVA foam 68–69
EZ screen *see* silk screening

fabric tube, turning out 25
fabric weight and stretchiness 47–48
floral pick(s) 87–89
floral stemming machine 85, 87–89
flute (glass) 109, 111
fractions, adding them 18–19

frame point driver 84–85
free-hand foot 28–29
french cleat 2–4
fugitive glue 64–66
furniture, building tolerances 21
furniture dimensions 11–13

G-code 98–100
gel stain 51–54
gel wax 74–76
glaze(s) 57, 60
glue block 6–7
greenware 72–75, 102, 145–146
grommet setter 90–93

half hitch 132
Henson stitch 24
highball glass 109
hot glue 63–65, 83
hurricane glass 109–110

ice/dessert wine bottle 114–115
image transfer methods 76–80
impulse sealer 10–11
Irish coffee glass 109–110

KISS, Keep it Simple Stupid 150–151
knots 131
Kreg jig 5

ladder stitch 24
large format printer 33, 95–99
laser engraver/cutter 103–105
lowball glass 109

margarita glass 109–110
marking fabric 28
martini glass 109–110
measurements, preciseness 21–22
metric conversion 11, 35

newspaper formats 119

old fashioned glass 109

paint brushes: pre-clean 55; reviving dried out ones 54–55
paint can lid management 50–51
paper, ageing/distressing 69–71
paper sizes, American 122–123
paper sizes, international 124–126
paper, softening 71–72
pattern matching 46–47
percentage, determining increase/decrease 14–18, 32–33
period 128–129
period styles 126–127
pilsner glass 109, 112
pint glass 109, 113
piping wrap: determining amount 34–36; making it 36–38
pleater hooks 40
pleater tape 40
pocket hole(s) 5
pocket screw(s) 5
port bottle 114
pounce(ing) 79
pounce wheel 79
power cord management 7–9
princess stitch 24
prop math 14
proportional math, examples 14–18
puff cigarettes 80–82

quick release fabric items 26–27

red wine glass 109, 111
rivet setter 90–91
rocks glass 109
roll hem foot 28–29
rose wine glass 109, 112

sealing wax 63–65
seam closing stitch 24–25
setting the proper table 115–119
sewing machine feet 28–29
shirring tape 40
shot glass 109–110
silk screening 56–59

sling glass 109, 113
slip 72–74
slip casting 72–75
snap tape 26–27
snifter (glass) 109–110
soft sculpture animals 32–33
sparkling wine bottle 114–115
sphere of fabric, creating one 30–31
spiking a tablecloth 30, 32
split-ring pliers 83–84
square knot 138–139
stein (glass) 109, 113
stretch wrap 9–10

T-shirt transfer 76–77
table setting: casual/basic 115–116; formal 115, 117–119; informal/semi-formal 115–117
tightening/loosening hardware 10–11
time periods *see* period styles

tool path 99, 101
truckers hitch 136–138
tulip glass 109, 113

units of measure 19–21
upholstery, quick method 48

vacuum form machine 92–97
Velcro 9, 26–27
vinyl: heat transfer 100; setting it 66–67; sticky back 97
vinyl cutting machine 100–102

wash(es) 57, 60–61
Weizen glass 109, 112
white wine glass 109, 112
wine bottle types 113–115
wood joints, fixing them 4–5

zipper/cording foot 28

For Product Safety Concerns and Information please contact our EU representative GPSR@taylorandfrancis.com
Taylor & Francis Verlag GmbH, Kaufingerstraße 24, 80331 München, Germany

www.ingramcontent.com/pod-product-compliance
Lightning Source LLC
Chambersburg PA
CBHW052121300426

44116CB00010B/1761